# STAR WARS

## IN 100 SCENES

WRITTEN BY
**JASON FRY**

# CONTENTS

## HOW TO USE THIS BOOK

*Star Wars in 100 Scenes: Experience the Excitement of the Epic Saga* tells the story (so far) of *Star Wars* scene by scene. Beginning with Episode I and ending with Episode VI, this guide selects iconic moments from each film, with stunning images illustrating key events and accompanying text detailing the tale's twists and turns, surprises and intrigues. Panels on the pages offer behind-the-scenes detail, while boxes spotlight key characters, vehicles, locations and droids the first time they appear.

## BEHIND-THE-SCENES

■ Throughout the book coloured panels like this one provide behind-the-scenes information about the making of the *Star Wars* films. These give a fascinating glimpse into the locations, actors and special effects used to create Episodes I to VI.

# A LONG TIME AGO IN A GALAXY FAR, FAR AWAY....

Life creates and nurtures the mysterious energy field known as the Force, which surrounds and binds everything in creation. Most beings are unaware that the Force exists, but a few can sense its will, and work with it in order to perform astonishing feats.

For a thousand generations the Jedi Knights have defended the galaxy's great Republic by channelling the Force for knowledge and peace. But the Republic has grown weak, rotted by political corruption, and too many of the Jedi have become set in their ways. They do not know that their ancient enemies – the evil order of dark side Force-users known as the Sith – are plotting to destroy all that the Jedi have protected for so long.

This is the story of how the Sith took their revenge, destroying the Jedi and transforming the Republic into an evil Galactic Empire. It is the tale of the mightiest of the Jedi – Anakin Skywalker, the Chosen One prophesied to bring balance to the Force.

It chronicles how Anakin was seduced by evil and fell into darkness, serving the Sith as Darth Vader. But it is also the story of Anakin's secret twin children: his daughter Leia, leader of the fight to restore the Republic, and his son, Luke, destined to reignite the Jedi flame and redeem his fallen father.

In their adventures, Luke and Leia will encounter remarkable friends and foes. The smugglers Han Solo and Chewbacca help fight the Empire's sinister servants, Jedi exiles Yoda and Obi-Wan Kenobi seek to foil the schemes of the Sith, and loyal droids C-3PO and R2-D2 try to help their masters out of the worst sorts of trouble. Luke and Leia must defeat the Empire's faceless stormtroopers, escape greedy crime lords such as Jabba the Hutt and, finally, confront Darth Sidious, the secret Dark Lord of the Sith who undermines the Republic and then rules the Empire. The story of the Skywalkers is also the saga of the galaxy, in which the fate of millions of planets is decided.

**THE GREEDY TRADE** Federation blockades the peaceful planet Naboo, turning a dispute over taxes into a political crisis for the Galactic Republic. Weary of endless debate in the Senate, the Republic's Supreme Chancellor Valorum secretly sends two Jedi Knights – Qui-Gon Jinn and his Padawan Learner Obi-Wan Kenobi – to end the dispute. But the Jedi are unaware that the Trade Federation is controlled by the Sith Lord Darth Sidious, or that the blockade is part of his sinister plan to take over the Republic.

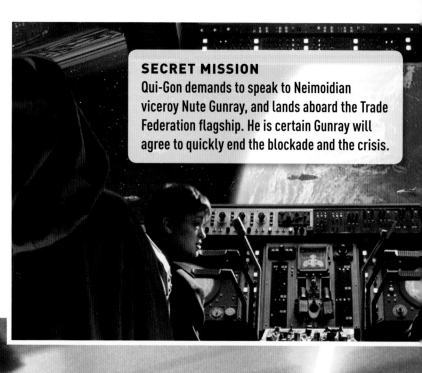

### SECRET MISSION
Qui-Gon demands to speak to Neimoidian viceroy Nute Gunray, and lands aboard the Trade Federation flagship. He is certain Gunray will agree to quickly end the blockade and the crisis.

## A PLOT REVEALED

> **"The negotiations will be short."**
> QUI-GON JINN

Obi-Wan's design for his lightsaber is similar to Qui-Gon's blade.

### NOTABLE CHARACTERS

| | | |
|---|---|---|
| Qui-Gon Jinn | Obi-Wan Kenobi | Nute Gunray |
| Rune Haako | Darth Sidious | Daultay Dofine |

## "KILL THEM IMMEDIATELY"

While Qui-Gon and Obi-Wan wait, the panicked Neimoidians contact Sidious. The Sith Lord tells them to kill the Jedi and invade Naboo.

## JEDI HUNT

The Neimoidians try to kill the Jedi with poison gas, but they are able to escape and try to cut through to the bridge. Deadly destroyer droids arrive and chase the Jedi through the Trade Federation ship.

## VEHICLES

Trade Federation Freighter

Republic Cruiser

Unaware of her masters' plot, TC-14 brings refreshments.

## FAMILY TIES

- Noted Scottish actress Lindsay Duncan supplies TC-14's voice. Her husband Hilton McRae plays an A-wing pilot in Episode VI.

- Ewan McGregor, who plays Obi-Wan, is the nephew of Denis Lawson, who plays Wedge Antilles in Episodes IV to VI.

## DROIDS

Battle Droid

Destroyer Droid

## LOCATION

Naboo

**OBEYING DARTH SIDIOUS'S** orders, the Trade Federation blocks communications to Naboo and lands an army of battle droids and war machines on the lush green world. As the ships arrive, creatures flee through the swamps in all directions. Qui-Gon and Obi-Wan stow away on a landing craft, determined to reach Naboo's capital city of Theed and warn the planet's ruler, Queen Amidala. Along the way, they pick up unexpected help when Qui-Gon rescues a clumsy Gungan exile named Jar Jar Binks.

### INVASION FORCE
As Qui-Gon and Obi-Wan watch from hiding, Trade Federation battle droids board huge landing craft and descend to Naboo.

# INVASION: NABOO

### NOTABLE CHARACTERS

Padmé Amidala

Jar Jar Binks

Captain Panaka

Sabé

Ikopi are mammals with long tongues that they use to grasp branches with tasty leaves.

### LONE LIAM
- The only live action featured in this scene is actor Liam Neeson running in swampy vegetation.

**THE PHANTOM MENACE**

## AMIDALA CAPTURED

The native Naboo are no match for the Trade Federation's droids, and offer little resistance. A triumphant Gunray enters Theed and tries to force the queen to sign an unfair treaty.

## AN UNEXPECTED MEETING

Hurrying to escape the Trade Federation's vehicles, Qui-Gon comes to the rescue of a terrified Gungan, Jar Jar Binks. Very grateful for Qui-Gon's help, Jar Jar offers to take the Jedi to his people's hidden underwater city – Otoh Gunga.

> "That is the sound of a thousand terrible things heading this way."
>
> QUI-GON JINN

Multi-Troop Transports (MTT) carry 112 battle droids in deployment ranks.

**VEHICLES**

MTT

STAP

C-9979 Landing Craft

**LOCATION**

Theed

**JAR JAR BRINGS** the Jedi to the underwater city of Otoh Gunga, where Qui-Gon asks the Gungan leader Boss Nass for help against the droid army. Nass refuses – his aquatic people dislike Naboo's human inhabitants. However, he agrees to give the Jedi a Bongo submarine and let them take Jar Jar as a navigator. It is not much of a favour: Nass knows that Jar Jar is accident-prone, and the underwater route to Theed is guarded by dangerous sea creatures that see a Gungan sub as a tasty snack to be devoured.

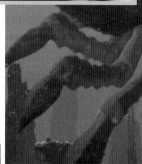

### INTO THE PLANET CORE
Boss Nass tells the Jedi that the fastest way to Theed is to go through Naboo's core, which is honeycombed with passages. That throws Jar Jar into a panic: many undersea predators have a lair in the shadowy depths of the core.

**NOTABLE CHARACTERS**

Boss Nass

Captain Tarpals

**LOCATION**

Otoh Gunga

# UNDERWATER ATTACK

## "There's always a bigger fish."
QUI-GON JINN

Bongos are built by a secret method, using organic and mechanical parts.

### TONGUE-TIED
Jar Jar is right to worry: an armoured opee sea killer spots the sub, catches it with its tongue and starts to reel in its prize.

### MONSTERS OF THE DEEP
The sea killer, with its sub snack, is caught by a mighty sando aqua monster, a huge predator of the Naboo depths. Luckily the vast sando stops to devour a colo claw fish, and the sub is able to race away to safety.

**VEHICLE**

Bongo

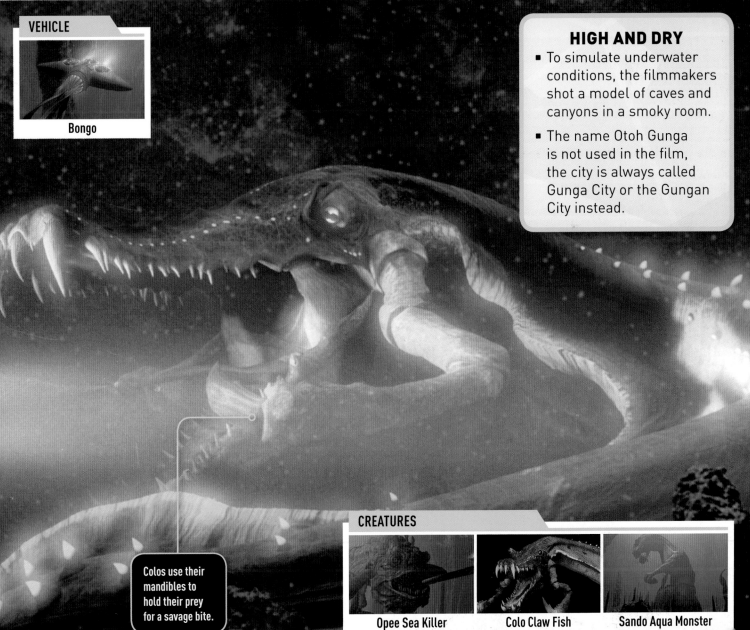

### HIGH AND DRY
- To simulate underwater conditions, the filmmakers shot a model of caves and canyons in a smoky room.
- The name Otoh Gunga is not used in the film, the city is always called Gunga City or the Gungan City instead.

Colos use their mandibles to hold their prey for a savage bite.

**CREATURES**

Opee Sea Killer

Colo Claw Fish

Sando Aqua Monster

**THE JEDI REACH** Theed in time to save Queen Amidala and her handmaidens from the Trade Federation's battle droids. Qui-Gon urges the queen to accompany the Jedi to Coruscant, the Republic's capital, and after a word with her handmaiden Padmé, the queen agrees. Qui-Gon and Obi-Wan fight their way past droids guarding the Royal Starship and take off. However, in order to reach safety, they still have to get past the deadly battleships of the Trade Federation, which are waiting in orbit above Naboo.

**DROID CROWDS**
Battle droids overwhelm opponents with their vast numbers, but they are no match for the combat skills of Jedi Knights. With blazing lightsabers, Qui-Gon and Obi-Wan dispatch their metal foes.

# FREEING THE QUEEN

### STRONG DESIGNS
- The original design for the Neimoidian masks was changed during production. The battle droids resemble mechanical versions of that original design.
- Though Darth Maul is a strong presence, he has only three lines in the whole film.

Battle droids take their orders from computers aboard the Droid Control Ship.

**NOTABLE CHARACTERS**

R2-D2

Darth Maul

Ric Olie

R2-N3

R2-M5

R2-B1

R2-R9

G8-R3

## ASTROMECHS UNDER FIRE

The queen's starship runs the blockade, but takes hits from the battleships. Astromech droids try to perform repairs while under fire. R2-D2 stands his ground and fixes the ship, enabling it to escape.

### DARK APPRENTICE

Disgusted by the queen's escape, Darth Sidious introduces his Sith apprentice, Darth Maul. He will find Amidala's ship.

## "You're under arrest!"

BATTLE DROID

| LOCATION | VEHICLE |
|----------|---------|
| Theed Royal Palace | Royal Starship |

One of the handmaidens follows events with special interest.

**THE QUEEN'S STARSHIP** is too damaged to reach Coruscant, so Qui-Gon heads instead to Tatooine, a desert planet ruled by the Hutt crime lords. Qui-Gon finds the parts they need at Watto's junk shop, where he also meets a young slave named Anakin Skywalker. Anakin is strong with the Force, and Qui-Gon comes up with a plan to win the parts and free Anakin from slavery. For the plan to work, Anakin must win the perilous Boonta Eve Podrace. The boy has never won such a race; in fact, he's never even finished.

**TALENT WITH THE FORCE**
Anakin brings Qui-Gon, Padmé, Jar Jar and R2-D2 home to meet his mother, Shmi. Qui-Gon is convinced that he has met Anakin through the will of the Force.

## RACE FOR FREEDOM

# "There is something about this boy."
QUI-GON JINN

**DROIDS**

Power Droid          Pit Droids

The Force enables Anakin to see things before they happen, giving him the amazing reflexes needed for podracing.

**COTTON CROWD**
- The crowd in the Mos Espa Arena includes a mix of live actors, CGI characters and painted cotton swabs, which fill out the highest rows of the stands.

**LOCATIONS**

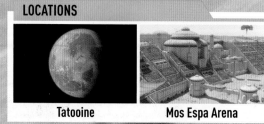

Tatooine          Mos Espa Arena

**I** THE PHANTOM MENACE

## THE BOONTA EVE RACE

Qui-Gon makes a wager: if Anakin wins the podrace, Watto must give Qui-Gon the parts he needs and free the boy. Watto isn't worried as he has bet heavily on a ruthless racer named Sebulba.

## RACE TO THE END

The race comes down to Anakin and Sebulba, who battle for the lead on the last lap. When Sebulba's pod crashes, Anakin streaks across the finish line.

Sebulba's engines are barely legal, and his podracer boasts hidden weapons for use when referees are not looking.

### VEHICLE

Podracer

### NOTABLE CHARACTERS

Anakin Skywalker

Watto

Shmi Skywalker

Sebulba

C-3PO

Jabba the Hutt

THOUGH DEVASTATED AT being separated from his mother, Anakin agrees to travel to Coruscant with Qui-Gon and train as a Jedi. The two leave Mos Espa to rejoin Obi-Wan and the others aboard the queen's starship. But Darth Maul has tracked the ship to Tatooine, and used his probe droids to find the Jedi. Sidious's apprentice leaps on his speeder and races across the blazing sands of Tatooine to attack Qui-Gon. He is eager to avenge the ancient defeat that forced the Sith to conceal their presence from the Republic.

**A SAD FAREWELL**
Qui-Gon tries to free Shmi as well as Anakin, but Watto refuses. Wanting a better life for her son, she gently tells him to go...and not look back. Anakin agrees, though the parting leaves him heartbroken.

# DARK ADVERSARY

## SITH SKILLS

- As a gymnast and martial-arts expert, actor Ray Park shaped much of Maul's acrobatic fighting style.

- Maul's horns were made of rubber for safety during Episode I's action scenes.

DRK-1 probes can be set to seek out individuals.

**"My guess is he was after the queen."**
QUI-GON JINN

## SERVING THE SITH
When the droids spot Qui-Gon, Maul hurries to intercept him, forcing the Jedi to fight for his life against a cunning warrior.

## FATEFUL MEETING
*Following a devastating duel, Qui-Gon escapes by leaping onto the ramp of the queen's ship. There he introduces Anakin to Obi-Wan. Their meeting will have enormous consequences for the galaxy.*

Facial tattoos are a tradition on Dathomir.

### DROID

Sith Probe Droid

### CREATURE

Eopie

### VEHICLES

*Scimitar* (Sith Infiltrator)   *Bloodfin* (Sith Speeder)

**ONCE ON CORUSCANT** Queen Amidala meets with Naboo's Senator Palpatine. He warns that Chancellor Valorum, cannot help despite being one of Naboo's strongest supporters – he is plagued by bureaucracy and political woes. Palpatine suggests that Amidala call for a Senate vote of "no confidence" in Valorum, which would lead to a Senate election for a new Chancellor. The queen is reluctant to betray an ally in this way, but her fear for her planet and her frustration with the Senate are growing.

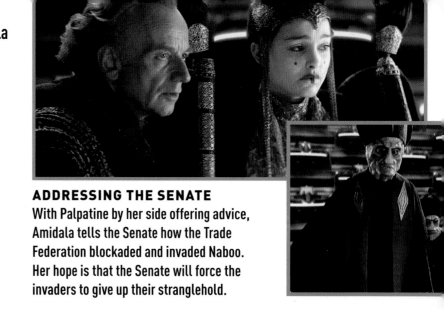

### ADDRESSING THE SENATE
With Palpatine by her side offering advice, Amidala tells the Senate how the Trade Federation blockaded and invaded Naboo. Her hope is that the Senate will force the invaders to give up their stranglehold.

## SENATE INTRIGUE

### NOTABLE CHARACTERS

Senator Palpatine

Chancellor Valorum

Lott Dod

Sei Taria

Mas Amedda

The 1,024 delegations each have a platform that undocks.

**DROID**

Cam Droid

**VEHICLE**

Air Taxi

## OBJECTION RAISED

The Trade Federation's Lott Dod asks for proof and suggests the Senate create a commission to look at Amidala's charges. The queen despairs of getting help.

## CRISIS AT THE TOP

Amidala takes Palpatine's advice and calls for a "no confidence" vote. The Republic will have a Supreme Chancellor. Who will it be?

Valorum's podium rises from his offices beneath the floor.

> "I was not elected to watch my people suffer and die while you discuss this invasion in a committee."
>
> QUEEN AMIDALA

## PHONE HOME

- Look closely to spot senators of the same species as E.T. from the 1982 film, *E.T. The Extra-Terrestrial*.

- Bail Organa of Alderaan was cut from this scene. Jimmy Smits played the character in Episodes II and III.

## LOCATIONS

Coruscant

Galactic Senate

Senate Chamber

QUI-GON TELLS THE Jedi Council about events on Naboo and the Sith warrior he fought on Tatooine. The Jedi have trouble believing the Sith have returned, and order Qui-Gon and Obi-Wan to return with Amidala to Naboo. Qui-Gon tells the Jedi he believes that Anakin is the Chosen One, prophesied to bring balance to the Force. Qui-Gon thinks the will of the Force brought them together, and is determined to train Anakin as a Jedi. Yoda and Mace Windu agree to test the boy, but think training him is unwise.

**TALES OF THE SITH**
The Jedi believe the Sith were defeated a thousand years ago, and doubt Qui-Gon's attacker was one of them. They tell Qui-Gon and Obi-Wan to guard Amidala while they ponder this mystery.

# FACING THE JEDI COUNCIL

Anakin is old to be trained as a Jedi. Most Jedi are trained when they are infants.

"The boy is dangerous – they all sense it. Why can't you?"
OBI-WAN KENOBI

**LOCATIONS**

Jedi Temple          Jedi Council Chamber

I   THE PHANTOM MENACE

## DEFYING THE COUNCIL
Qui-Gon rejects the warnings from the Council and Obi-Wan that Anakin is dangerous and cannot be trusted. Qui-Gon will follow the will of the Force, as he always has, and knows that Anakin is meant to become a Jedi.

## ANAKIN'S TEST
The Jedi test Anakin and find the Force is strong with him. But they also decide he is too old and has formed emotional attachments, which Jedi avoid. They sense that fear and anger cloud his judgment, and forbid Qui-Gon to train him.

## NOTABLE CHARACTERS

Yoda

Mace Windu

Ki-Adi-Mundi

Plo Koon

Saesee Tiin

Adi Gallia

## ABOVE IT ALL
- This set was built at a height of 1.8 m (6 ft) above the floor because several Jedi – including the theatrical release's Yoda – were puppets operated from below.

Yoda has the highest rank of the 12 Jedi on the Jedi Council.

AMIDALA RETURNS TO Naboo despite Qui-Gon's warning that the Jedi can protect her, but not fight for her. She asks Jar Jar Binks to bring her to the Gungans, who are hiding in the swamps. In the Gungan Sacred Place, Boss Nass refuses the queen's request for an alliance, but is surprised when a royal handmaiden, called Padmé, steps forward. Padmé admits she is the real queen – the other is a decoy used in times of danger – and drops to one knee to beg for help. Moved by her gesture, Nass agrees to go to war against the droids.

**THE QUEEN'S REQUEST**
The Gungans think Naboo's humans are arrogant and selfish, but Padmé's humble gesture shows Nass they can be friends.

# SEEKING ALLIES

**LOCATION**

Gungan Sacred Place

The stone heads of the Gungan Sacred Place were made centuries ago.

"Our fate is in your hands."

PADMÉ AMIDALA

I THE PHANTOM MENACE

## DARK LORD'S ORDERS
When Darth Sidious hears the Gungans are on the march, Amidala's boldness surprises him. He tells Darth Maul and Nute Gunray to advance and destroy the Gungan army.

## ASSEMBLING AN ARMY
Padmé asks the Gungan army to lure the droids away from Theed. That will let her raid the city and capture the Trade Federation's Nute Gunray while starfighters strike the Droid Control Ship, disabling the droid army.

The long earlobes of Gungans are used to display their emotions.

### VEHICLE

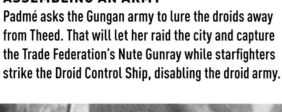

Flash Speeder

## FAMILIAR FACE?
- Padmé's decoy, whose name is Sabé, is played by British actress Keira Knightley, who starred in the film trilogy *Pirates of the Caribbean*.

**THE GUNGANS EMERGE** from the swamps, mounted on their kaadus and defended by energy shields carried on the backs of massive fambaas. Jar Jar and his old friend Captain Tarpals are among the leaders as the Gungans march onto the Great Grass Plains. Confronting them is Nute Gunray's droid army, which has left Theed and is deploying from racks inside massive MTTs. The droids march towards the Gungans' protective shields, laser rifles at the ready. The fight for Naboo has begun!

### PRESENT ARMS!
The Gungan clans are capable fighters. Infantry use catapults to hurl plasma energy balls at the enemy, the cavalry attack with double-bladed electropoles and the action is coordinated by drums and horns.

# THE BATTLE FOR NABOO

## "Ouch time!"
### CAPTAIN TARPALS

### SEEMS FAMILIAR?
- This scene was shot near Livermore, California, with the hills digitally stretched to look less Earthlike.
- Recordings of pigs' grunts and whales' breaths were used for the sounds of the kaadus.

Gungan militia shields are held in one hand or strapped to the forearm.

## HOLD THE LINE
The droids march through the protective shields and target the shield generators on the backs of the hulking fambaas. The Gungan militia fire up their shields and prepare for close combat.

### TECHNOLOGICAL THREAT
Battle droids deploy from MTTs after a Trade Federation artillery barrage fails to bring down the Gungans' shields.

### LOCATION

**Great Grass Plains**

### CREATURES

**Kaadu**

**Fambaa**

**Falumpaset**

Battle droids use brute force to overwhelm their enemies.

**AS THE DROID** army battles the Gungans, Padmé, the Jedi and several Naboo soldiers slip into Theed to capture Nute Gunray. Their first stop is the royal hangar, where they defeat a squad of battle droids. The fighter pilots fly off to attack the Droid Control Ship, with Anakin taking refuge in the cockpit of a starfighter. But the intrusion has been detected: Darth Maul enters the hangar, double-bladed lightsaber at the ready. Qui-Gon and Obi-Wan ignite their blades and advance on the tattooed Sith warrior.

### DARK-SIDE DEFENDER
Maul has spent his entire life learning to harness his rage and use it to focus the power of the dark side of the Force. He is eager for a rematch with the Jedi, burning to prove himself in battle against them.

Qui-Gon knows he cannot match the younger Maul's stamina, and has to stay calm and draw on the Force for strength.

## JEDI VS SITH

**I** THE PHANTOM MENACE

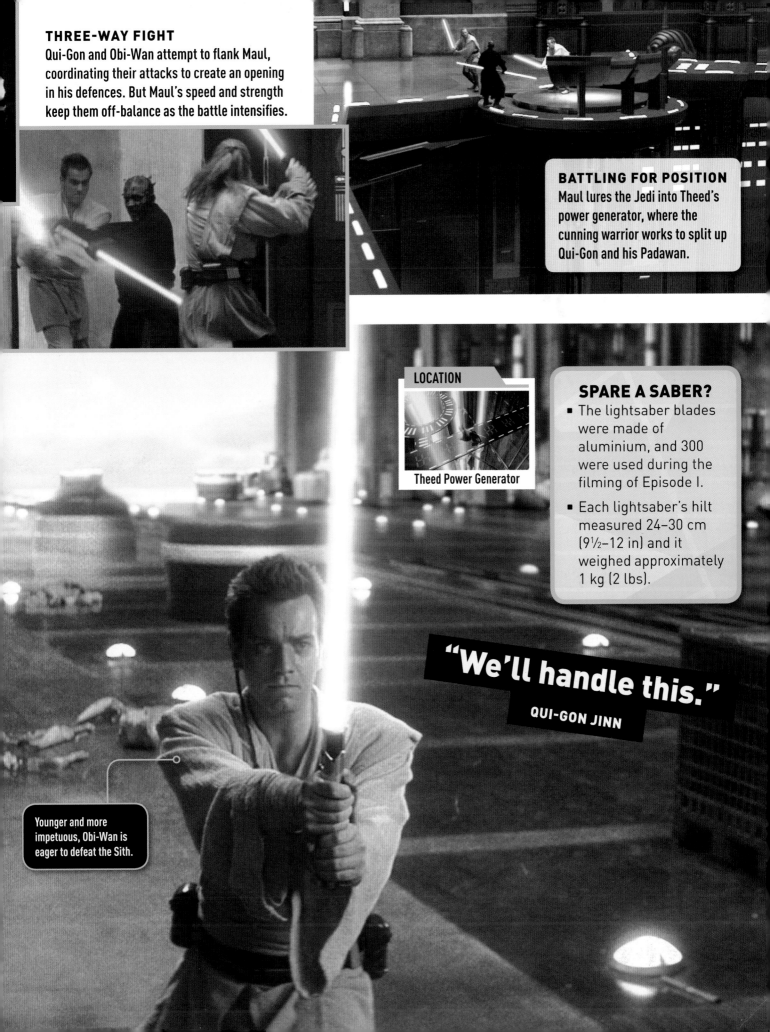

## THREE-WAY FIGHT

Qui-Gon and Obi-Wan attempt to flank Maul, coordinating their attacks to create an opening in his defences. But Maul's speed and strength keep them off-balance as the battle intensifies.

### BATTLING FOR POSITION

Maul lures the Jedi into Theed's power generator, where the cunning warrior works to split up Qui-Gon and his Padawan.

**LOCATION**

Theed Power Generator

### SPARE A SABER?

- The lightsaber blades were made of aluminium, and 300 were used during the filming of Episode I.
- Each lightsaber's hilt measured 24–30 cm (9½–12 in) and it weighed approximately 1 kg (2 lbs).

## "We'll handle this."

QUI-GON JINN

Younger and more impetuous, Obi-Wan is eager to defeat the Sith.

AS THE JEDI duel with Maul, Padmé, her handmaidens and Captain Panaka fight their way deeper into the palace, trying to reach Nute Gunray in the throne room. Padmé and her decoy, Sabé, split up and fight running battles with Gunray's defenders through the palace's elegant marble halls. By capturing Gunray, Padmé hopes to end the Trade Federation's brutal occupation of Naboo and force the viceroy to sign a new treaty – one that will make him pay for his inhumanity and his crimes against a peaceful planet.

**GOING UP!**
Pinned down by battle droids, Padmé's raiders break through a window and use their ascension guns to zip up to the next floor, bypassing an entire wave of droids protecting the Trade Federation viceroy.

# RETAKING THE PALACE

**NOTABLE CHARACTERS**

Eirtaé    Rabé

**VEHICLE**

Gian Speeder

As head of royal security, Panaka oversees the Security Guard, Palace Guard and Space Fighter Corps.

## SURROUNDED
Padmé's band is surrounded in the throne room, but when Gunray sees Sabé, he thinks she is the real queen and sends most of his forces after her, allowing Padmé to turn the tables and capture him.

## HUNT IN THE HALLS
To confuse their foes, Padmé and Panaka go one way, while Sabé (dressed as the queen) goes another. Battle droids chase both groups.

## ROYAL DUEL
- The Naboo palace scenes were shot in southern Italy's 18th-century Reggia di Caserta.
- In this scene, Padmé's blaster makes the sound of a .44 Magnum.

Like many diplomats and dignitaries, Padmé has as her weapon of choice, a lightweight but powerful ELG-3A pistol.

# "We must not fail to get the viceroy. Everything depends on it."
**PADMÉ AMIDALA**

**ON THE GREAT** Grass Plains, the battle droids of the Trade Federation break the lines of the Gungan army, and the fight turns into a wild free-for-all. Jar Jar and Captain Tarpals are caught in the chaos as AAT tanks and destroyer droids join battle droids in chasing bands of fleeing Gungans. Jar Jar hastily surrenders when he and Tarpals are cornered, to the Captain's dismay. But no sooner does Jar Jar throw up his hands than the droids halt and slump over, deactivated and helpless.

**SHIELDS DOWN**
With the Gungan shield generators down, the AAT tanks join the fight, chasing down the Gungans and their mounts.

**THX TRIBUTE**
- One of the battle droids' backpacks says 1138. This is a reference to *THX-1138*, George Lucas's first feature film.

When the signal from the Droid Control Ship ceases, the battle droids power down, becoming metal statues.

# THE GUNGAN GENERAL

### A FRIEND IN NEED
Captain Tarpals arrives on his kaadu with a plasma ball, and Jar Jar uses the energy ball to short-circuit the tank. Battle droids surround the Gungans, who need a miracle – and get one when starfighters destroy the Droid Control Ship. Who was the heroic pilot?

### OVER A BARREL
Predictably, Jar Jar is in the middle of all the trouble. Through luck and his usual misadventures he destroys many battle droids, but somehow winds up clinging to the gun barrel of a speeding Trade Federation tank!

## "Dey all broken!"
### JAR JAR BINKS

Whiskers like Captain Tarpals's are a sign of maturity among the Gungans.

### VEHICLE
AAT Battle Tank

DURING THE JEDI raid on the palace on Theed, Anakin's choice of a fighter cockpit as a hiding place turns out to be a good one, as he guns down several destroyer droids threatening his friends. But he accidentally engages the autopilot, and the fighter zooms out of the hangar and into space. Unable to go back, Anakin joins the battle between Amidala's pilots and the droid starfighters of the Trade Federation. It's even more exciting than podracing, and technically he is obeying Qui-Gon's order that he "Stay in that cockpit!"

## DANGEROUS GAME
As R2-D2 beeps frantically, Anakin struggles to figure out the unfamiliar controls of his fighter. He needs all his piloting skills and a little help from the Force to survive the savage dogfight above Naboo.

# AN UNLIKELY HERO

## BRAVO, JOHN!
- Visual effects supervisor, John Knoll, has a cameo in this scene as Bravo 4.
- At least 3,000 boys auditioned for the part of Anakin.

Anakin wears a helmet left behind by Essara Till (Bravo 7).

## BELLY OF THE BEAST

Hit by a blast from a droid starfighter, Anakin spins out of control and plunges into the hangar of the Droid Control Ship. His fighter overheats and shuts down, and battle droids rush to capture him.

## SAVING THE DAY

Anakin fires at the droids and misses, but hits the Droid Control Ship's main reactor, starting a chain reaction that destroys it.

### NOTABLE CHARACTERS

Porro Dolphe (Bravo 2)

Arven Wendik (Bravo 3)

Rya Kirsch (Bravo 4)

Dineé Ellberger (Bravo 5)

### VEHICLES

Naboo Starfighter

Droid Control Ship

### DROID

Vulture Droid

## "I'll try spinning. That's a good trick."
ANAKIN SKYWALKER

A readout in Anakin's fighter translates R2-D2's beeps, allowing the droid and Anakin to communicate.

**MEANWHILE,** in the Theed Palace, Darth Maul cleverly separates Qui-Gon and Obi-Wan. Obi-Wan watches in shock from behind a laser wall as Maul defeats his Master, leaving Qui-Gon mortally wounded. Maul then outduels Obi-Wan, disarming him and leaving him clinging to a beacon above a seemingly endless drop. However, a gloating Maul is blinded by his own arrogance. Obi-Wan summons his fallen Master's saber, Force-leaps from the pit and cuts the Sith warrior in two.

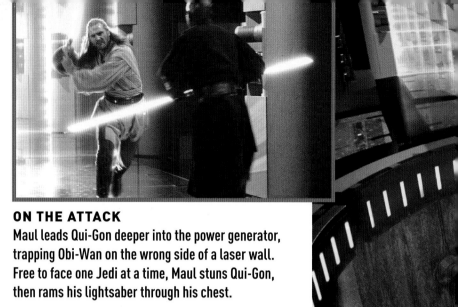

### ON THE ATTACK
Maul leads Qui-Gon deeper into the power generator, trapping Obi-Wan on the wrong side of a laser wall. Free to face one Jedi at a time, Maul stuns Qui-Gon, then rams his lightsaber through his chest.

**SABER SHOWDOWN**

**LOCATION**

Power Generator Core

Jedi wear simple clothes and carry minimal gear, relying on their resourcefulness and the Force.

## QUI-GON'S NOBLE END
With the aid of the Force, Obi-Wan leaps from the pit and cuts Maul in half. With his last breath, Qui-Gon asks Obi-Wan to promise that he will take Anakin as his Padawan Learner.

### MAUL'S TRIUMPH
Obi-Wan attacks Maul in a frenzy, but the wily Sith bests him as well, leaving Obi-Wan hanging on by his fingertips in a deep pit.

The design of Maul's saberstaff is based in part on an ancient Zabrak weapon called a zhaboka.

### MAUL APPEARS
- Two actors have voiced Darth Maul – Peter Serafinowicz in Episode I and Sam Witwer in *Star Wars: The Clone Wars* TV show.

- *The Clone Wars* revealed that Maul survived being cut in two, returning to challenge Obi-Wan Kenobi and confront Darth Sidious.

# "Promise me you'll train the boy. He is the Chosen One."
QUI-GON JINN

**ANAKIN'S DESTRUCTION** of the Droid Control Ship ends the Trade Federation's hopes of winning the fight for Naboo, and Nute Gunray is arrested and taken to Coruscant for trial. The Jedi hold a solemn funeral for the fallen Qui-Gon Jinn, while Yoda and Mace Windu wonder how to deal with the mysterious return of the Sith. But the people of Naboo celebrate: their planet has been freed, and a new era of peace has begun, one that will unite the planet's human and Gungan citizens.

**A NEW CHANCELLOR**
Naboo's Senator Palpatine is now the Chancellor of the Republic, and promises that he will watch Anakin's career with great interest.

# NABOO CELEBRATION

**LOCATION**

Funeral Temple

**VEHICLE**

Star Shuttle

**FORESHADOWING**
- The celebration is similar to the one that ends Episode IV, with a Skywalker hero and R2-D2 looking on.

Anakin now wears the traditional clothes and cropped hair of a Jedi, with a Padawan's short braid.

**A JEDI'S DOUBTS**
Yoda grants Obi-Wan the rank of Jedi Knight, and honours Qui-Gon's last wish by letting him serve as Anakin's Master. But he warns Obi-Wan that he senses enormous danger in training the boy.

**THE NEW PADAWAN**
Anakin knows little of Yoda's fears, and has never been happier. Once a slave on Tatooine, he has now helped Padmé save her planet, proved himself as a pilot and won a place in the Jedi Order.

The Globe of Peace is a Naboo relic of blown glass encasing a sphere of plasma.

**"Always two there are...a Master and an apprentice."**
YODA

**TEN YEARS AFTER** the Battle of Naboo, thousands of systems are planning to leave the Republic and join the Separatist movement of former Jedi Count Dooku, causing turmoil in the Senate and straining the Jedi Order's ability to keep the peace. Responding to the threat, some senators seek to create an army for the Republic. Padmé Amidala, once Naboo's queen and now its senator, opposes the plan, fearing it will lead to war. She rushes back to Coruscant for the debate, but someone tries to silence her when she arrives.

## ARRIVAL ON CORUSCANT

Guarded by starfighters, Padmé's royal cruiser lands on a platform high above Coruscant. Down the lowered ramp comes Cordé, a handmaiden of Padmé who is serving as a decoy for her mistress.

# A SENATOR IN PERIL

### CHANGE OF DUTIES

- On Naboo, the queen is elected to her position. By having Padmé step down between Episode I and Episode II, George Lucas emphasised that the Republic is a democracy.

Gregar Typho succeeded his uncle Captain Panaka as Padmé's head of security.

## SNEAK ATTACK
Suddenly, an explosion rips the gleaming starship apart. Disguised as a fighter pilot, Padmé rushes to Cordé's side – but it is too late.

## MEETING THE CHANCELLOR
The Jedi and Chancellor Palpatine think spice miners on Naboo were behind the assassination attempt. But Padmé thinks the assassin wanted to silence a voice for peace, and blames Dooku.

| LOCATION | VEHICLE | NOTABLE CHARACTERS | | |
|---|---|---|---|---|
|  |  |  |  |  |
| Chancellor's Office | Royal Cruiser | Senator Amidala | Chancellor Palpatine | Captain Typho |

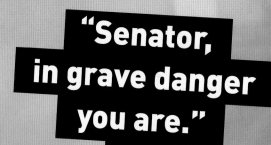

## "Senator, in grave danger you are."
YODA

Padmé's handmaiden Cordé, as well as another named Versé, die in the blast, but her chief handmaiden, Dormé, survives.

**PALPATINE ASKS THAT** Obi-Wan Kenobi and his Padawan, Anakin Skywalker, protect Padmé from further attempts on her life. Anakin is tongue-tied at the sight of the beautiful young woman he has loved since first seeing her years ago on Tatooine, and he promises her that he and Obi-Wan will find her attackers. While the Jedi stand guard, the bounty hunter Zam Wesell sends an assassin droid after Padmé, leading to a harrowing speeder chase across the busy aerial traffic lanes of the Republic capital.

### NIGHT ATTACK

While Padmé sleeps, an assassin droid cuts a hole in her window and releases two poisonous kouhuns. The deadly creatures escape R2-D2's notice, but Anakin and Obi-Wan sense the threat and rush to her defence.

## SPEEDER CHASE

### COLOUR CAMEO

- Anakin's speeder shares a bright yellow finish with the '32 Deuce Coupe (licence plate THX 138) in Lucas's film *American Graffiti*.

### NOTABLE CHARACTERS

Anakin Skywalker

Jango Fett

Zam Wesell

Dormé

Elan Sleazebaggano

## HANG ON!
Obi-Wan grabs the droid as it flees Padmé's room, clinging to it high above Coruscant's skyscrapers. Anakin follows in a borrowed airspeeder, rescuing his Master and recklessly chasing after Zam.

## HUNTER SILENCED
The Jedi capture Zam in the Outlander Club, but a mysterious figure shoots her with a poison dart before she reveals who hired her.

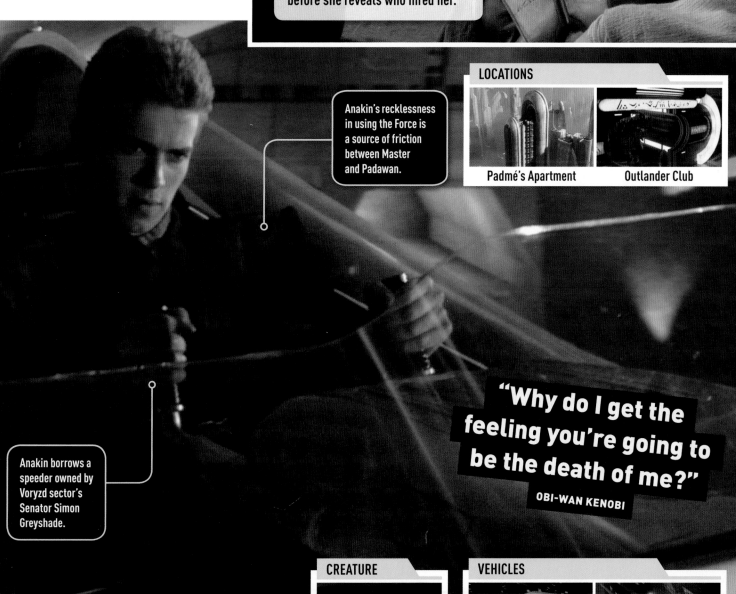

Anakin's recklessness in using the Force is a source of friction between Master and Padawan.

### LOCATIONS

Padmé's Apartment

Outlander Club

Anakin borrows a speeder owned by Voryzd sector's Senator Simon Greyshade.

> "Why do I get the feeling you're going to be the death of me?"
> OBI-WAN KENOBI

### CREATURE

Kouhun

### VEHICLES

XJ-6 Airspeeder

Koros-2 Airspeeder

**THE LONE CLUE** to the identity of Zam's killer is the poison dart used to silence her. After the Jedi Order's research droids fail to identify the dart, Obi-Wan brings it to his friend Dexter Jettster, who has been from one end of the galaxy to the other. Dex identifies the weapon as a saberdart from Kamino, a world known for creating clones. But Obi-Wan now faces a new mystery. The Jedi Archives are the galaxy's greatest library, filled with the Order's accumulated wisdom. So why is there no listing for Kamino?

### AN OLD FRIEND
Dex tells Obi-Wan that the dart was made on Kamino, located beyond the galaxy's Outer Rim, near the Rishi Maze.

# SEARCH FOR THE LOST WORLD

### CLASSY ROOM
- The Jedi Council Chamber was reused as the younglings' training room, with the floor pattern changed and columns and plants added.

Obi-Wan's holographic map includes the main galaxy and companion galaxies such as the Rishi Maze.

**VEHICLE**

Jedi Starfighter

## "Lost a planet, Master Obi-Wan has. How embarrassing!"
YODA

## A CHILD'S WISDOM
When Obi-Wan asks Yoda for help, one of the younglings has the answer: Kamino does exist, but someone erased it from the Archives. To find out why, Obi-Wan decides to visit the lost world.

## JEDI KNOWLEDGE
To Obi-Wan's surprise, the Jedi Archives show no planet located at those coordinates. Librarian Jocasta Nu tells Obi-Wan that if an item does not appear in the Archives' records, it does not exist.

Kamino's erasure disturbs Obi-Wan: since only Jedi have access to the Archives, one of his fellow Jedi must have deleted the file about it.

### NOTABLE CHARACTERS

Jocasta Nu

Dexter Jettster

WA-7

Hermione Bagwa

### LOCATIONS

Dex's Diner

Jedi Archives

**OBI-WAN FINDS** Kamino right where the coordinates predicted it would be – and is surprised to hear that the Kaminoans are expecting him. To his shock, he learns that the cloners have spent a decade growing and training a huge army of clones from the DNA of a bounty hunter named Jango Fett. The Republic had not voted to create an army for its own defence, but the army exists anyway. So who paid the cloners to make it? And who erased it from the Jedi Archives to hide their secret project?

### MYSTERIOUS ORDERS

The Kaminoans think Obi-Wan is here to inspect the army they created on orders from the Jedi Master Sifo-Dyas. But Obi-Wan has never heard of such an order – and Sifo-Dyas was reported killed on Felucia a decade earlier.

# PLANET OF THE CLONES

### NOTABLE CHARACTERS

| Lama Su | Taun We | R4-P17 |
| --- | --- | --- |

Clone armour is colour-coded by rank. This trooper's red markings show that he is a captain.

### FATHER OF THE ARMY

The Kaminoan Taun We says the soldiers are clones of a bounty hunter named Jango Fett, who lives on the planet. Remembering that a Kaminoan saberdart killed Zam, Obi-Wan asks to meet Fett.

### IDENTICAL SOLDIERS

Touring the army facilities, Obi-Wan watches thousands of soldiers – all of them clones – take part in drills preparing them for battle.

Troopers pick up gear and receive new training diagnostics from central computer terminals like this one.

### UFO SIGHTING?

- The aliens from Steven Spielberg's 1977 film *Close Encounters of the Third Kind* helped inspire the design of the Kaminoans.

## "This army is for the Republic."

LAMA SU

### LOCATIONS

Kamino

Tipoca City

### CREATURE

Aiwha

WHILE OBI-WAN investigates the attacks on Padmé, she and Anakin travel to Naboo disguised as peasants and stay at her home in the Lake Country. In this peaceful setting Anakin gives in to his romantic feelings for the senator, and now that she is free from worries about politics, Padmé finds herself falling in love with her Jedi bodyguard. Ordinarily, a senator has little time for romance, and the Jedi code forbids emotional attachments. But as Padmé and Anakin discover, love is rarely convenient.

**LOVE AT THE LAKE**
At Varykino, Anakin can no longer keep his feelings hidden, and he kisses Padmé as they gaze out over the beautiful lake. Though she knows it is not a good idea, she cannot resist the moment and kisses him back.

# FORBIDDEN ROMANCE

> ## "We could keep it a secret..."
> ### ANAKIN SKYWALKER

As a Jedi from a desert world, Anakin finds it odd to picnic on lush Naboo. But he is too infatuated with Padmé to feel out of place.


y

z

w

v

u

t

II ATTACK OF THE CLONES

46

## A COZY SETTING
Padmé tells Anakin that their love affair must end. Unable to bear the idea, he suggests they hide their relationship from the galaxy.

## IN THE MEADOWLANDS
Padmé knows she and Anakin cannot marry: the Jedi Order would expel him, and Naboo's queen would recall her from the Senate. But they cannot resist their feelings, and fall in love anyway.

## ROMANTIC VISTAS
- The Lake Country scenes were shot in and near Italy's Villa Balbianello. The picnic was shot in a meadow near the villa, then combined with footage and visual effects of waterfalls and a matte painting.

Away from the Senate and Naboo's capital of Theed, Padmé welcomes the chance to escape her planet's formal dress code.

### LOCATION
Varykino

### CREATURE
Shaak

### VEHICLES
Gondola Speeder

Airbus

**OBI-WAN MEETS** Jango Fett and his son, Boba (who is actually a perfect clone created by the Kaminoans). Jango refuses to say if he has been on Coruscant recently, but Obi-Wan catches sight of his Mandalorian armour, and is sure it was Jango who killed bounty hunter Zam Wesell. He tries to capture Jango, battling him on a landing platform with blasters blazing and lightsaber flashing. The duel between Jedi and bounty hunter is a draw, and the Fetts flee in their starship *Slave I* – but Obi-Wan has a way to follow them.

### TENSE MEETING

When Obi-Wan asks about the Jedi Master Sifo-Dyas who supposedly ordered the creation of the army, Jango tells Obi-Wan he has never heard of him. He says a man named Tyranus hired him to provide his DNA for clones. Yoda and Mace Windu tell Obi-Wan to capture Jango and bring him to them for questioning.

## JANGO'S ESCAPE

### WET WEATHER

- The ceiling-mounted rain system developed for the fight pumped in seven and a half tonnes of water per minute.

Jedi use a form of combat called Shien to deflect blaster bolts back at an attacker, turning a defensive move into an attack.

> **"I'm just a simple man trying to make my way in the universe."**
>
> **JANGO FETT**

## BATTLE IN THE RAIN
Suspicious of the Jedi, Jango tells Boba to pack his things – they are leaving. Obi-Wan tries to stop him, and the two duel in the rain. It is an even match: neither man is able to gain the upper hand.

## HUNTER'S ESCAPE
Jango flings Obi-Wan off the platform, and seizes the moment to escape in *Slave I* – but not before the Jedi attaches a tracker to his ship.

**NOTABLE CHARACTER**

Boba Fett

**VEHICLE**

*Slave I*

The Jedi defeated Mandalore's warriors centuries ago, and armour like Jango's is now a rare sight in the galaxy.

THE TRACKER ATTACHED to *Slave I* enables Obi-Wan to follow Jango and Boba to the ringed world of Geonosis. But the bounty hunter's ship has sensitive instruments, and the Fetts soon discover that they are being followed. They attack Obi-Wan, peppering his starfighter with laser blasts, missiles and deadly seismic charges that turn the chunks of rock in the planetary rings into dangerous projectiles. Obi-Wan needs all of his piloting skills just to survive the encounter.

**ENEMY SIGHTED**
A wise bounty hunter is alert to pursuit, and the Fetts are quick to spot Obi-Wan's fighter on *Slave I*'s tail.

## "This is why I hate flying!"

OBI-WAN KENOBI

The Delta-7 *Aethersprite* fighter is customised with powerful engines and pinpoint steering suitable for Force-aided reflexes.

# DUEL IN THE RINGS

## A SEISMIC SURPRISE

With Obi-Wan proving a stubborn opponent, Jango reveals a final surprise: potent weapons known as seismic charges. The charges implode, then redirect that energy outwards in massive shock waves.

## THE PURSUER PURSUED

Looping around in the rings, Jango catches Obi-Wan unawares, and unleashes a furious barrage of laser fire at the Jedi pilot. Even with help from R4-P17, Obi-Wan barely evades the hunter.

*Slave I*'s repulsorlift wings and cockpit rotate between vertical flight mode and horizontal landing mode.

**LOCATION**

Geonosis

## SOUND OF SILENCE

- Sound designer Ben Burtt calls the sound of the seismic charge an "audio black hole", in which the sonic blast follows a moment of silence.

WHILE STAYING ON Naboo with Padmé, Anakin has a vision that his mother, Shmi, is in danger. He and Padmé leave for Tatooine, where Anakin discovers Shmi has married a moisture farmer named Cliegg Lars – and was recently kidnapped by savage Tusken Raiders. Anakin searches the desert wastes for his mother. His quest ends in grief and pain, leading to rage fuelled by the dark side of the Force. The episode is a glimpse of the future: Anakin's inability to master his emotions will lead to tragedy for himself and those he loves.

### DESERT QUEST

Cliegg Lars says Shmi has been gone for a month, and there is little hope she is still alive. But Anakin can feel his mother's presence in the Force, and is determined to use his powers to save her.

# TRAGEDY ON TATOOINE

## "I killed them. I killed them all."

ANAKIN SKYWALKER

Anakin's suffering creates a disturbance in the Force so powerful that Yoda feels it halfway across the galaxy on Coruscant.

### LOCATIONS

Mos Espa

Lars Farm

**II** ATTACK OF THE CLONES

## A SON'S RAGE

Anakin finds his mother in a Tusken camp, but she dies in his arms. Overwhelmed by pain and rage, he slaughters the Tusken men, women and children, then returns to the Lars's farm carrying Shmi's body.

## DARK PROMISE

Anakin tells Padmé what he has done, and vows to grow so strong with the Force that he will be able to stop people from dying.

## NOTABLE CHARACTERS

Cliegg Lars

Owen Lars

Beru Whitesun

## VEHICLES

Zephyr-G Swoop

Naboo Yacht

In later years Cliegg Lars's son, Owen, removes the headstones from the family graves, leaving them unmarked.

## FAMILIAR HAUNTS

- For these scenes, the Lars's "igloo" home from Episode IV was rebuilt in the Tunisian desert, with the Sidi Driss Hotel in the town of Matmata used again for interior shots.

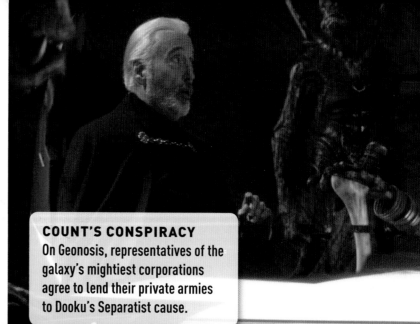

**ESCAPING THE FETTS,** Obi-Wan lands on Geonosis and discovers Count Dooku and the Separatist leaders making plans to fight the Republic. He contacts the Jedi and reveals the plot, but is captured. Word of the threat throws the Senate into turmoil, and none other than Jar Jar Binks proposes giving emergency powers to Chancellor Palpatine. The fateful decision allows Palpatine to use the clone army created by the Kaminoans. War is coming, and it will soon engulf the galaxy.

**COUNT'S CONSPIRACY**
On Geonosis, representatives of the galaxy's mightiest corporations agree to lend their private armies to Dooku's Separatist cause.

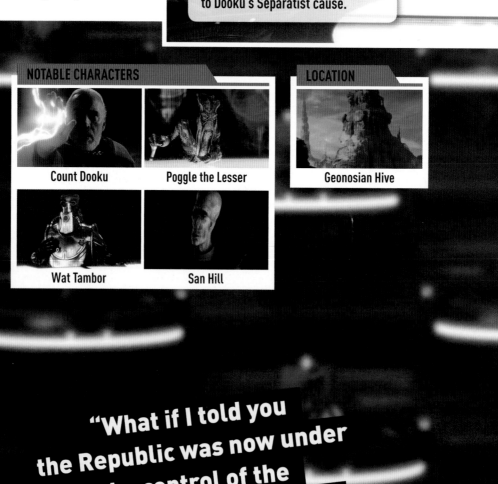

**NOTABLE CHARACTERS**

Count Dooku

Poggle the Lesser

Wat Tambor

San Hill

**LOCATION**

Geonosian Hive

# PREPARING FOR WAR

"What if I told you the Republic was now under the control of the Dark Lords of the Sith?"
COUNT DOOKU

**II** ATTACK OF THE CLONES

## JAR JAR'S MOMENT
With Padmé away from Coruscant, Representative Binks speaks for Naboo. Thinking he is doing the right thing, Jar Jar proposes an amendment giving Palpatine the power to create a great Republic army.

## A TERRIBLE TRUTH
Dooku tells the captive Obi-Wan that a Sith Lord named Darth Sidious controls the Senate. Obi-Wan thinks that is a lie, but Dooku ought to know: his secret identity is Darth Tyranus, Sidious's apprentice.

## SCREEN LEGENDS
- Christopher Lee, who plays Dooku, co-starred with Episode IV's Peter Cushing (Grand Moff Tarkin) in many horror films of the 1950s.

The Chagrian Mas Amedda is Speaker of the Senate, and one of the few beings in the galaxy to know some of Palpatine's darkest secrets.

An Umbaran, Sly Moore serves Palpatine as staff aide, and is rumoured to be able to influence minds.

**ANAKIN IS ORDERED** to stay on Tatooine and protect Padmé at all costs, despite word of Obi-Wan's captivity on nearby Geonosis. Padmé decides she will rescue Obi-Wan herself, and if Anakin wants to protect her he will have to come along. Accompanied by R2-D2 and C-3PO, the two race to Geonosis, where they discover the planet's factories are working overtime making battle droids. Other dangers await: Padmé is walking right into the clutches of Nute Gunray, the Separatist who hired Jango Fett to assassinate her.

### "MACHINES CREATING MACHINES"

Padmé and Anakin hope to rescue Obi-Wan from the Separatists, but find themselves trapped in an automated Geonosian assembly line. If they are not careful they will wind up stamped, or melted – or both.

## MISSION TO GEONOSIS

### LATE ADDITION

- Originally, Anakin and Padmé were arrested after negotiations with Dooku failed. The droid factory scene was added after Lucas decided something more dramatic was needed.

- The actors in this scene were shot in a single morning, with everything else created using miniatures and computer graphics.

- Anakin and Padmé find themselves trapped on a retracted bridge, much like Luke and Leia in Episode IV.

Safety is not a priority in the factory, and many Geonosian drones have been maimed or killed by mould-stampers.

## "Don't move, Jedi!"

JANGO FETT

**PROTOCOL PERIL**
While R2-D2 rescues Padmé, C-3PO wanders into the assembly line where battle droid parts are put together.

**DOOKU'S PRISONERS**
Anakin escapes a messy end on the assembly line, but his lightsaber is cut in two. Defenceless, Anakin is no match for Jango Fett and a party of destroyer droids. They capture him and Padmé.

With so much activity and machinery around him, Anakin is at a disadvantage in trying to detect danger.

**LOCATION**
Geonosian Factory

**DROID**
Forklift Droid

**TO THE DELIGHT** of Nute Gunray, the Geonosians sentence Padmé and Anakin to death for espionage. As they are brought into the gladiatorial arena, Padmé tells Anakin she loves him and they share a last kiss. The two are chained next to Obi-Wan, who is also awaiting execution. As excited Geonosian drones cheer, three savage monsters enter the arena – a nexu, an acklay and a reek. But the Geonosians are robbed of their blood sport when the captives free themselves and fight.

## ON TOP OF THINGS

A sleek-furred, vicious nexu leaps at Padmé, who is wounded by its claws. But the Naboo senator scrambles atop her execution pillar and uses the heavy chain as a weapon against her attacker.

## JEDI CAPTURED

### RAY'S WAY

- Obi-Wan's duel with the acklay is a tribute to the 1961 film, *Mysterious Island*, which features sailors fighting a giant crab animated by special effects master Ray Harryhausen.

**LOCATION**

Geonosian Arena

**CREATURES**

Nexu

Reek

Acklay

Orray

## JEDI UNCHAINED

Facing the needle-sharp teeth of an acklay, Obi-Wan goads the creature into battering down his pillar, then grabs a spear from a dead Geonosian guard. Now the odds are more even!

## REEK RIDER

Anakin evades a charge from the rampaging reek, then uses the Force to calm the enraged animal, turning it into his mount.

Soldier drones, all of which have wings, are one of the castes that make up the Geonosians' strict hive society.

Beast-battles known as "petranaki" are a common Geonosian method for executing prisoners, and attract huge crowds.

## "I've got a bad feeling about this."

**ANAKIN SKYWALKER**

**THE THREE CAPTIVES** fight bravely, but are hopelessly outnumbered. All appears lost – until Mace Windu arrives with dozens of lightsaber-wielding Jedi. The Geonosians counter by unleashing their droid army, leading to a wild battle. One by one the Jedi fall to droid attacks, and Dooku calls on the survivors to surrender. Windu refuses, and the droids raise their blasters – but are destroyed by gunships, swooping down from the skies with weapons blazing. Yoda and the clone army have joined the fight!

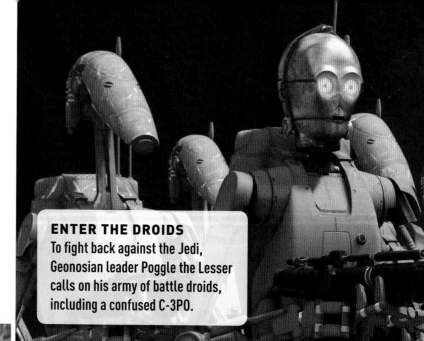

### ENTER THE DROIDS
To fight back against the Jedi, Geonosian leader Poggle the Lesser calls on his army of battle droids, including a confused C-3PO.

# ARENA BATTLE

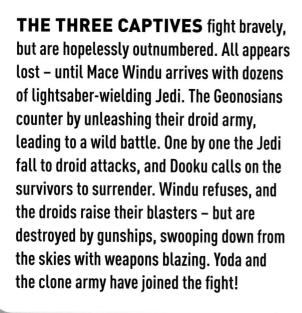

To save credits, battle droids are outfitted with normal blasters, not more expensive built-in weapons.

### SIDE MISSION
- Scenes in which Ki-Adi-Mundi and Plo Koon lead a Jedi raid on a Separatist Droid Control Ship were shot but cut before visual effects were added.

## CLONE RESCUE
Not even the Force can overcome hopeless odds, and the Jedi survivors are surrounded. All appears lost, but Yoda arrives from Kamino, leading the mysterious clone army into battle against Dooku's battle droids.

## ORPHANED BY WAR
The arriving clones rescue the Jedi, and Dooku retreats as the arena battle becomes a rout. In the aftermath of the fight, young Boba Fett mourns the loss of his father Jango, struck down by Windu.

## "This party's over."
MACE WINDU

200 Jedi were recruited to join Mace Windu's rescue mission.

### DROID
Super Battle Droid

### VEHICLE
Assault Gunship

## NOTABLE CHARACTERS
Shaak Ti

Coleman Trebor

Kit Fisto

Aayla Secura

Luminara Unduli

Barriss Offee

**THE FIGHT IN THE ARENA** is just the beginning: Republic AT-TE walkers and artillery storm across the Geonosian plains, accompanied by clone infantry and given cover by airborne gunships. Count Dooku orders his droid armies to fight back as the corporations of the Separatist alliance try to evacuate their grounded starships. Battle droids trade fire with clone troopers, as droid vehicles charge into the fight. Explosions rattle the hives where the Geonosians dwell as missiles shriek through the air.

## SEPARATIST RETREAT

The Separatist leaders know the Republic army is too big to defeat in open battle. They send droids to slow the clone advance while Separatist crews load starships and make preparations to escape into orbit.

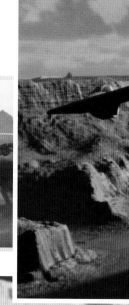

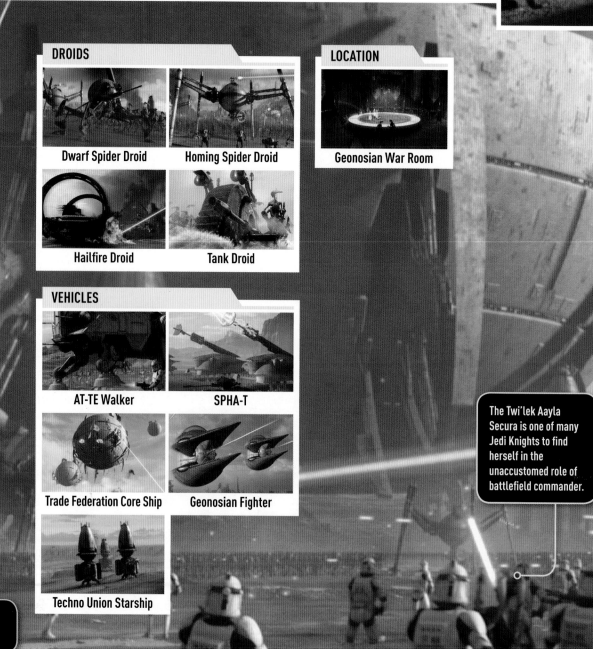

### DROIDS

Dwarf Spider Droid

Homing Spider Droid

Hailfire Droid

Tank Droid

### LOCATION

Geonosian War Room

### VEHICLES

AT-TE Walker

SPHA-T

Trade Federation Core Ship

Geonosian Fighter

Techno Union Starship

The Twi'lek Aayla Secura is one of many Jedi Knights to find herself in the unaccustomed role of battlefield commander.

**STRIKE FORCE**
The Republic tries to prevent the Separatists' escape. Gunships lead the assault as ground forces advance with artillery units.

**NEW LEADERSHIP**
The Jedi see themselves as peacemakers, not warriors. But on Geonosis they must serve as generals for the hastily assembled army, fighting alongside clones in the smoke and chaos of battle.

> "My Master will not let the Republic get away with this treachery."
>
> COUNT DOOKU

The spherical cores of the Trade Federation battleships detach from their cargo arms and engine blocks when they land on a planet.

**SENSE OF HISTORY**
- Concept design supervisors Erik Tiemens and Ryan Church studied World War II and Vietnam War footage for design inspiration for this battle.

**DOOKU FLEES THE BATTLE**, pursued by Anakin and Obi-Wan. The Jedi catch him in his secret hangar, but Dooku overcomes them with his Sith powers – only the arrival of Yoda saves them from destruction. After a furious lightsaber duel with his old Master, Dooku escapes, rushing to Coruscant to meet Darth Sidious. All is going as the Sith Lord planned it: the Republic now has a massive army, the first shots have been fired in a devastating galactic war and Dooku possesses the plans for a planet-killing weapon called the Death Star.

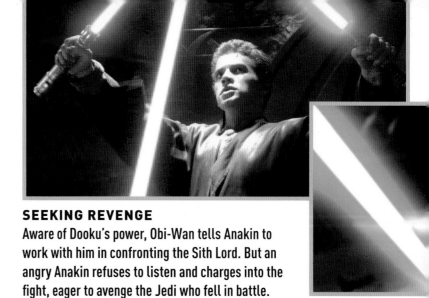

### SEEKING REVENGE

Aware of Dooku's power, Obi-Wan tells Anakin to work with him in confronting the Sith Lord. But an angry Anakin refuses to listen and charges into the fight, eager to avenge the Jedi who fell in battle.

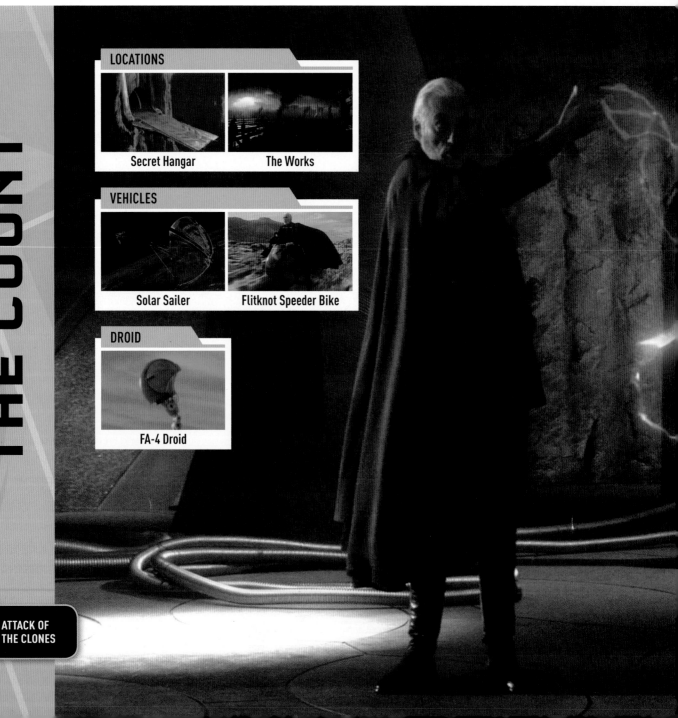

**LOCATIONS**

Secret Hangar

The Works

**VEHICLES**

Solar Sailer

Flitknot Speeder Bike

**DROID**

FA-4 Droid

# CONFRONTING THE COUNT

## OLD MASTERS

It is a poor decision: Dooku severs Anakin's hand and defeats Obi-Wan. Yoda arrives just in time to save the lives of the two Jedi.

## DARK SIDE DIVERSION

Yoda looks frail, but the Force is his ally: he fights Dooku in a dazzling acrobatic display. Dooku uses the Force to hurl debris at the fallen Anakin and Obi-Wan, then flees while Yoda prevents a column from crushing his friends.

Powerful Sith such as Dooku can manipulate the Force to create lightning that causes excruciating pain and drains life.

## DIGITAL JEDI

- The acrobatics required for this fight were impossible for a physical puppet, so the animators created an entirely digital Yoda.

Anakin lost his own lightsaber in the droid foundry, and so fights with a spare given to him by a Jedi during the arena battle.

## "Powerful you have become, Dooku. The dark side I sense in you."

YODA

**IT SEEMS AS** if the Republic has won a great victory. A grand army now defends it against the Separatists, and troops march aboard warships on Coruscant, headed for battlefields across the galaxy. Chancellor Palpatine and his allies in the Senate watch this display of military might in quiet awe, but others are disturbed by recent events. The galaxy is at war and the dark side clouds the Jedi's understanding of the many events. Dangerous activities have been set in motion, and no one knows what lies ahead.

## REPORTING FOR DUTY

As powerful senators watch from a reviewing stand, legions of clone troopers receive their orders and board assault ships, ready to fight the mechanical malice of the Separatists' armies.

# BEGUN, THE CLONE WAR HAS

Rodia's Onaconda Farr, an old friend of Padmé's, was a leading advocate of creating a Republic army.

## GALACTIC SUNSET

- The red light of sunset lends this scene an appropriate mood of foreboding, given what lies ahead in Episode III.

**II** ATTACK OF THE CLONES

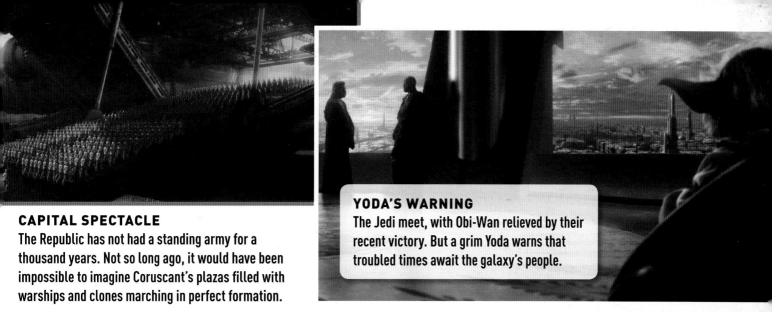

## CAPITAL SPECTACLE
The Republic has not had a standing army for a thousand years. Not so long ago, it would have been impossible to imagine Coruscant's plazas filled with warships and clones marching in perfect formation.

### YODA'S WARNING
The Jedi meet, with Obi-Wan relieved by their recent victory. But a grim Yoda warns that troubled times await the galaxy's people.

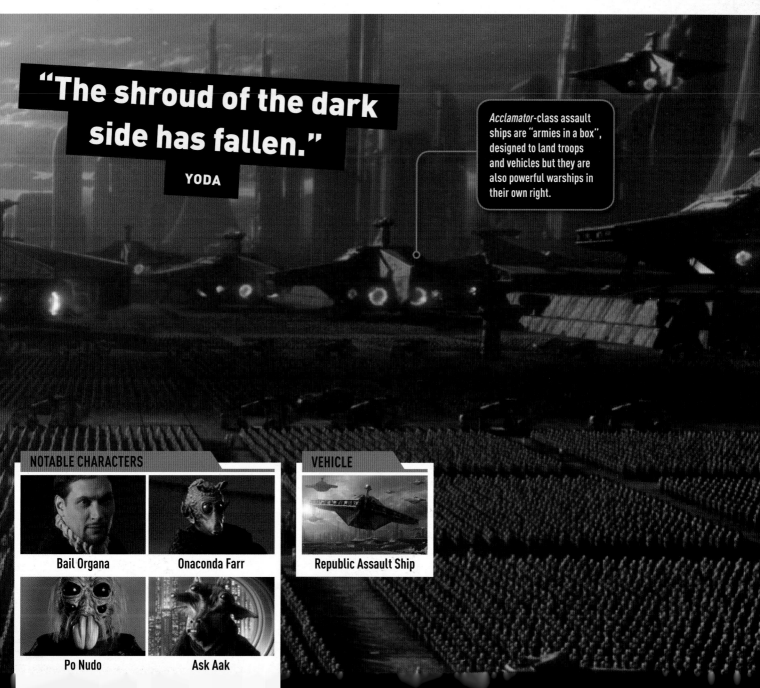

# "The shroud of the dark side has fallen."

**YODA**

*Acclamator*-class assault ships are "armies in a box", designed to land troops and vehicles but they are also powerful warships in their own right.

## NOTABLE CHARACTERS

Bail Organa

Onaconda Farr

Po Nudo

Ask Aak

## VEHICLE

Republic Assault Ship

**ANAKIN RETURNS** to Naboo with Padmé. The Jedi has been through many trials, and has a constant reminder of his failure against Dooku in his mechanical hand. He struggles to control his passions and his amazing power with the Force. He knows his heart, however, and loves Padmé more than anything in the galaxy. No longer able to deny her feelings, Padmé agrees to marry Anakin, though he is violating the Jedi Code and will be forced to leave the Order if their secret marriage is discovered.

## BITTERSWEET BRIDE

Padmé has always dreamed of a wedding day in the Lake Country. She regrets that neither her family nor friends can attend the ceremony, but at least she is at Varykino, her favourite place on her homeworld.

## SECRET MARRIAGE

### NOTABLE CHARACTER

Pontifex Agolerga

### SIMPLE SOLUTION

- After rejecting exotic fabrics, costume designer Trisha Biggar made Padmé's dress out of a bedspread found in an Australian antique shop.

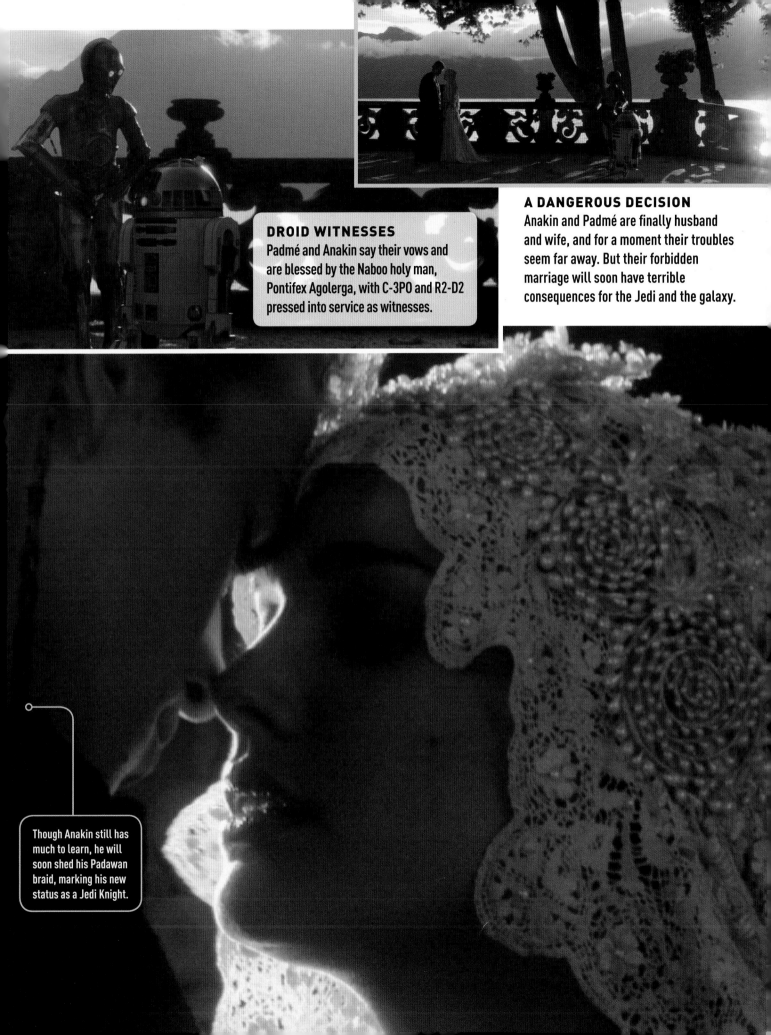

### DROID WITNESSES
Padmé and Anakin say their vows and are blessed by the Naboo holy man, Pontifex Agolerga, with C-3PO and R2-D2 pressed into service as witnesses.

### A DANGEROUS DECISION
Anakin and Padmé are finally husband and wife, and for a moment their troubles seem far away. But their forbidden marriage will soon have terrible consequences for the Jedi and the galaxy.

Though Anakin still has much to learn, he will soon shed his Padawan braid, marking his new status as a Jedi Knight.

AFTER THREE YEARS of grinding war against the droid armies of Dooku's Separatists, the Republic is finally close to victory. But the Separatist commander General Grievous launches a daring raid on the Republic capital world of Coruscant, kidnapping Chancellor Palpatine. Anakin and Obi-Wan race through hyperspace to the Chancellor's rescue and are caught in a savage battle, zooming through squads of droid starfighters as they struggle to reach Grievous's flagship, the *Invisible Hand*.

**INTO BATTLE**
Anakin and Obi-Wan emerge from hyperspace to find Republic and Separatist fleets exchanging fire in Coruscant's upper atmosphere.

# WAR OVER CORUSCANT

## "Here's where the fun begins."

ANAKIN SKYWALKER

Jedi cruisers engage the Separatists at point-blank range, with many ships destroyed.

III REVENGE OF THE SITH

## "FLYING IS FOR DROIDS"

Though an expert pilot, Obi-Wan hates flying – he'd rather let his astromech handle it. But Anakin is having fun, and uses his mastery of the Force to outfox the fighters defending Grievous's ship.

## BUZZ DROID ATTACK!

Buzz droids swarm the Jedi fighters, piercing their armoured hulls and destroying Obi-Wan's astromech, R4-P17. But R2-D2 is tougher prey, driving off the attackers with his fusion welder.

Debris plunges through the atmosphere, raining down on terrified Republic citizens.

### HEROIC APPROACH

- Episode III opens with a long "tracking shot", with a single camera following the Jedi starfighters into the thick of battle and ending with a close-up of R2-D2.

**DROID**

Buzz Droid

**VEHICLES**

ARC-170 Starfighter

Jedi Cruiser

**COUNT DOOKU** is the public leader of the Separatists and the secret apprentice of the Sith Lord Darth Sidious. He knows a terrible secret: Sidious and Chancellor Palpatine are the same person, and the Clone Wars are a Sith plot to take over the Republic. As Sidious's apprentice, Dooku thinks he will one day succeed his Master as ruler of the galaxy. But Dooku is wrong. His Master has betrayed him, as the Sith so often do. His fate is to be replaced by a younger, more powerful apprentice.

## WORKING TOGETHER

Anakin and Obi-Wan reach the tower on the *Invisible Hand* where Palpatine is pretending to be imprisoned. His captor, Dooku, expects to defeat the Jedi as he did on Geonosis. But Anakin is now far more powerful.

# DOOKU DEFEATED

> ## "Chancellor Palpatine, Sith Lords are our specialty."
> ### OBI-WAN KENOBI

## VEHICLES

*Invisible Hand*

Banking Clan Frigate

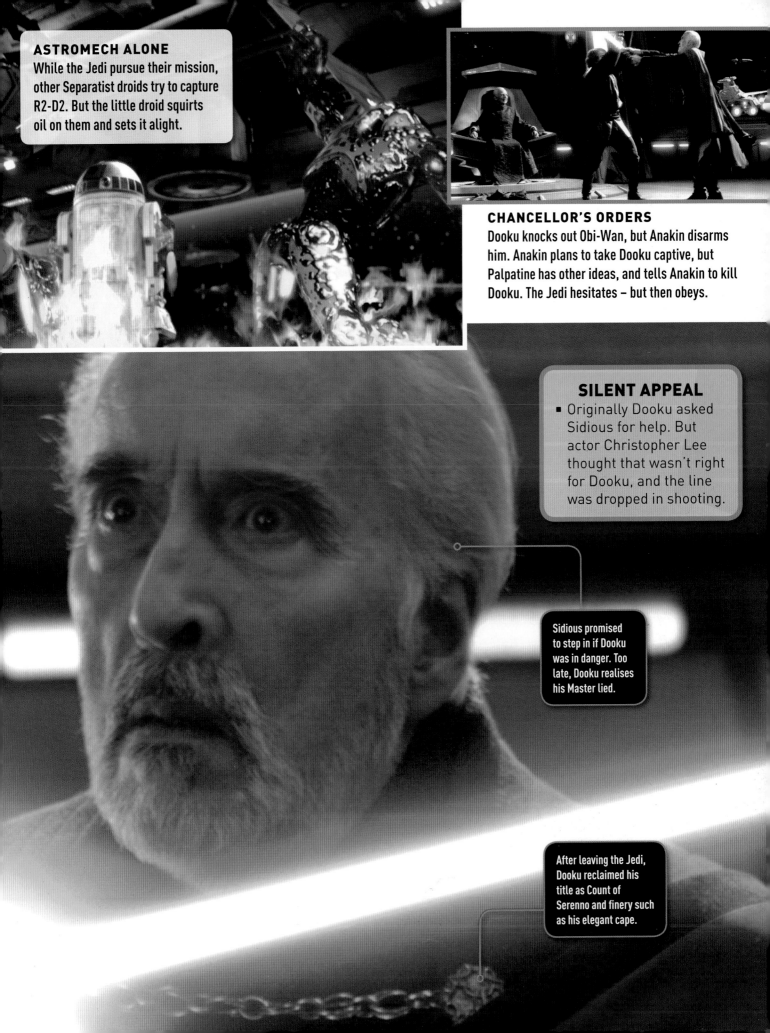

**ASTROMECH ALONE**
While the Jedi pursue their mission, other Separatist droids try to capture R2-D2. But the little droid squirts oil on them and sets it alight.

**CHANCELLOR'S ORDERS**
Dooku knocks out Obi-Wan, but Anakin disarms him. Anakin plans to take Dooku captive, but Palpatine has other ideas, and tells Anakin to kill Dooku. The Jedi hesitates – but then obeys.

**SILENT APPEAL**
- Originally Dooku asked Sidious for help. But actor Christopher Lee thought that wasn't right for Dooku, and the line was dropped in shooting.

Sidious promised to step in if Dooku was in danger. Too late, Dooku realises his Master lied.

After leaving the Jedi, Dooku reclaimed his title as Count of Serenno and finery such as his elegant cape.

THE JEDI HAVE rescued Palpatine, but are still trapped aboard the *Invisible Hand*, which is filled with battle droids and traps set by her owner, the vicious cyborg warlord known as General Grievous. A cruel and pitiless opponent, Grievous hates the Jedi and has tried to become their equal by replacing much of his body with mechanical parts. His ruthless battle fleets have ravaged Republic worlds and he has killed the Jedi sent to defeat him. Now Grievous wants Anakin and Obi-Wan for his next victims.

### R2-D2'S DIVERSION
Grievous's droid troops capture the Jedi, Palpatine and R2-D2 and bring them to the bridge. On a signal from Anakin, R2-D2 creates a diversion, allowing the Jedi to grab their lightsabers and fight.

# BATTLING WITH GRIEVOUS

**VEHICLE**

Firespeeder

Beneath his mask Grievous is a reptilian Kaleesh with few remaining organic parts.

Grievous keeps lightsabers inside his cape as trophies of the Jedi he has slain in battle.

> "Your lightsabers will make a fine addition to my collection!"
> GENERAL GRIEVOUS

III REVENGE OF THE SITH

## CAPTIVES OF GENERAL GRIEVOUS

The Jedi fight Grievous and his deadly MagnaGuards in a clash with sabers and electrostaffs. When the fight turns against him, Grievous flees and launches all of the ship's escape pods – including the one he escapes in himself.

## LOOK OUT BELOW

Battered by laser fire, Grievous's ship begins to break up. Anakin must guide her down to Coruscant for a perilous emergency landing.

## LOST JEDI

- Originally, the Jedi followed the Jedi Shaak Ti's homing beacon to Grievous's ship. Grievous executed Shaak in a scene cut from the film.

**DROID**

MagnaGuard

**NOTABLE CHARACTER**

General Grievous

**ON CORUSCANT, ANAKIN** is reunited with Padmé, whom he has secretly married. She tells him she is pregnant, a piece of happy news at a time when Anakin finds his loyalties tested. Palpatine makes Anakin his emissary to the Jedi Council, which the Jedi allow – but they refuse to grant him the rank of Jedi Master, and ask him to spy on the Chancellor. Worse, Anakin dreams of Padmé dying in childbirth. He had a similarly prophetic vision before his mother's death, and swears he will learn how to stop this one from becoming real.

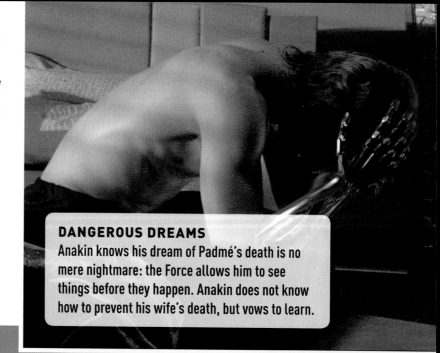

### DANGEROUS DREAMS
Anakin knows his dream of Padmé's death is no mere nightmare: the Force allows him to see things before they happen. Anakin does not know how to prevent his wife's death, but vows to learn.

### SQUID LAKE
- Anakin meets Palpatine at the Galaxies Opera House, where Mon Calamari dancers perform a ballet called "Squid Lake".

Anakin has told Yoda of his premonitions, without admitting his secret. Yoda's advice was to let go of all he fears losing.

# DIVIDED LOYALTIES

### LOCATION

Galactic Opera House

## A TANTALIZING TALE
Palpatine tells Anakin that the Sith Lord Darth Plagueis had the power to create life – and stop his loved ones from dying. Desperate to learn more, Anakin is unaware he is being drawn into a Sith plot.

## ANAKIN'S FRUSTRATION
Anakin is granted a seat on the Jedi Council, but he is refused the rank of Master – denying him access to lore he thinks could save Padmé.

## "It's very dangerous, putting them together."
MACE WINDU

Padmé hopes to have the baby in Naboo's Lake Country, where the birth can be kept secret.

**THE JEDI COUNCIL** learns that Grievous is hiding on the planet Utapau, and sends Obi-Wan to bring the Separatist warlord to justice. While clone forces wait in an orbiting Republic cruiser, Obi-Wan descends to the surface in his starfighter, and discovers that Grievous's battle droids are holding the Utapauans hostage. Obi-Wan confronts Grievous in front of legions of his droids. He is hopelessly outnumbered, but the Force is with him – and he intends to seize this chance to end the Clone Wars.

## BOLD CHALLENGE

Obi-Wan watches as Grievous herds the fugitive Separatist leaders into a getaway ship to hide elsewhere in the Outer Rim. Then he drops to the deck, challenging Grievous in front of his droid bodyguards.

# SHOWDOWN ON UTAPAU

Obi-Wan knows Grievous's rage makes him careless in battle – he will take risks to try to overwhelm his opponents.

## LOCATIONS

Utapau

Kashyyyk

**III** REVENGE OF THE SITH

**"Hello there!"**
OBI-WAN KENOBI

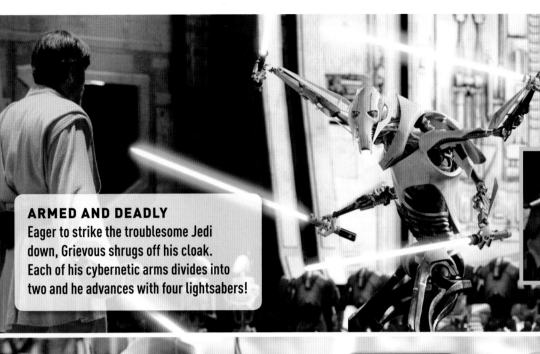

## MASTER OF THE FORCE
Each lightsaber is a whirling circle of doom in Grievous's hands – and now he has four of them. Obi-Wan cannot match his foe's speed or power, but he has the Force to guide him in battle.

### ARMED AND DEADLY
Eager to strike the troublesome Jedi down, Grievous shrugs off his cloak. Each of his cybernetic arms divides into two and he advances with four lightsabers!

Grievous claims he altered his body voluntarily, and thinks his cybernetic limbs are improvements.

### DIVIDE BY TWO
- For this scene actor Ewan McGregor fought a stunt double and had to react to an imaginary second pair of arms. Lucas decided to have Grevious quickly lose two hands to make the rest of the fight easier to choreograph.

## NOTABLE CHARACTERS

Chewbacca

Tarfful

Commander Cody

Commander Gree

R4-G9

Tion Medon

## VEHICLES

Droid Gunship

Ornithopter

Turbo Tank

**CLONE TROOPERS** invade Utapau, blasting away at Grievous's defenders. When the general flees on a wheel-bike, Obi-Wan leaps onto the back of an eager varactyl named Boga and gives chase. The two adversaries race through the tunnels and caverns of Utapau, scattering wide-eyed inhabitants as they go. Grievous hopes to reach his starfighter and escape the planet, but Obi-Wan heads him off, setting the stage for a final confrontation between the two old enemies.

**INVASION: UTAPAU**
Commander Cody and his clones storm Utapau's sinkholes, meeting stiff resistance from crab droids, Tri-droids and other mechanical monstrosities. But the battle-hardened clones soon gain the upper hand.

## DEATH OF A GENERAL

**CREATURE**

Varactyl

Brain implants improved Grievous's coordination, but made him angry and more aggressive.

Chest plates hide a sac containing Grievous's vulnerable internal organs.

## CAVERN CHASE
Boga easily keeps up with Grievous's wheel-bike, allowing Obi-Wan to wrestle with the cyborg. After a high-speed struggle, Obi-Wan knocks General Grievous from his getaway craft.

## ENEMY TERMINATED
Obi-Wan wrenches open the armour protecting Grievous's internal organs. Picking up a blaster, Obi-Wan brings the Separatist general's career to an end as Grievous bursts into flames.

## "So uncivilised!"
**OBI-WAN KENOBI**

### DROIDS

Crab Droid

Tri-Droid

### VEHICLES

Wheel-Bike

Grievous's Fighter

## PLAYING WITH FIRE
- In 2006, toymaker Hasbro created an entertainingly grisly action figure of Grievous. It depicted the moment of his demise, complete with plastic flames.

**ONCE OBI-WAN** has located Grievous, the Jedi decide they will remove Palpatine from office if he fails to give up his emergency powers at the end of the war. Anakin informs Palpatine that Grievous has been found, and then to his astonishment Palpatine offers to teach him the ways of the dark side of the Force and save Padmé's life. Anakin realises his mentor is the Sith Lord the Jedi have searched for. He tells Mace Windu, who gathers a team of Jedi to arrest Palpatine. However, capturing a Sith Lord is no easy assignment.

### CHANCELLOR'S CONFESSION
When Anakin discovers Palpatine's secret, he wants to strike down the Sith Lord, but he fears that the secret of how to save Padmé will die with him. Instead he decides to turn Palpatine over to the Jedi.

# PALPATINE'S SECRET

An expert starfighter pilot, Saesee Tiin has served on the Jedi Council for many years.

### FINALLY FIGHTING
- Episode III was actor Ian McDiarmid's fourth time playing Palpatine/Sidious but the first time he got to fight with a lightsaber.

## MACE'S MISSION

Sensing Anakin's fear and confusion Windu orders him to remain at the Jedi Temple. At the Chancellor's office, Sidious cuts down Jedi Saesee Tiin, Agen Kolar and Kit Fisto, using his dark-side powers.

## SITH LORD REVEALED

Mace Windu survives Sidious's savage attack, and begins to duel with the Chancellor. He does not know that Anakin is racing back to Palpatine's office, terrified that the Sith Lord's death will also seal Padmé's fate.

## "You are under arrest, Chancellor."

MACE WINDU

The Nautolan Jedi Kit Fisto is a veteran of battles on Geonosis, Vassek, Mon Cala and Lola Sayu.

### NOTABLE CHARACTER

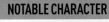

Agen Kolar

**ANAKIN ARRIVES AT** Palpatine's office to find Mace Windu and the Chancellor locked in combat. Windu disarms Sidious, who fights back with Force lightning, pleading for Anakin to help him and reminding him that he has the power to save Padmé. A desperate Anakin rescues Sidious and pledges to do all the Sith Lord asks in return for learning how to prevent his wife's death. Sidious accepts his new apprentice and gives him a Sith title: Anakin will now be called Darth Vader.

## SWORD OF THE JEDI

Mace Windu knows both the Jedi and the Republic stand on the verge of ruin, and has cornered the Sith Lord who caused so much pain. He will destroy Sidious in order to end the threat to the galaxy.

Force lightning rebounding from Windu's saber leaves Sidious's face scarred and disfigured.

As Darth Vader, Anakin now serves Darth Sidious. At any one time, only two Sith may use the title of "Darth" – the current Master and his or her apprentice.

## ANAKIN'S FALL

### REPUBLIC JUSTICE
Windu declares that the Sith Lord is too dangerous to be allowed to stand trial. To Anakin's horror, he raises his lightsaber for the killing blow.

### "YOU MUST CHOOSE"
The killing blow never lands. Anakin steps forward and severs Windu's hand, allowing Sidious to blast his attacker and send him plummeting from the building to his death. Anakin has made a fateful choice for himself and the galaxy.

## "Rise, Lord Vader."
**DARTH SIDIOUS**

### WEATHER AND SABERS
- To keep the views out of the windows of Coruscant consistent, the art department made detailed charts keeping track of day and night and even the ebb and flow of the city-planet's traffic.

- Mace Windu's lightsaber is the only one in the *Star Wars* saga with a purple blade, a distinctive touch requested by actor Samuel L. Jackson. While Windu made his debut in Episode I, he did not ignite his lightsaber on-screen until Episode II.

THE NEXT STEP in Darth Sidious's plan is to destroy the Jedi before they learn what has happened on Coruscant. Sidious has prepared for this day, and tells the clone commanders to carry out Order 66, which requires them to turn their weapons on their Jedi generals. Acting on a secret protocol implanted at the earliest stages of their development, the clones obey. The Jedi are badly outnumbered and taken by surprise, and so can mount little defence. Within minutes, ambushes across the galaxy kill thousands of members of the Jedi Order.

## CODY'S COMMAND

On Utapau, Commander Cody receives the order and opens fire on Obi-Wan and his varactyl. The blast sends Obi-Wan falling into the water far below. Cody orders his troops to search for the fallen Jedi.

## EYE-CATCHING COVER

- Dark Horse Comics introduced the character Aayla Secura. She was added to Episode II after George Lucas saw her featured on the cover of a comic book. The role was played by ILM production assistant Amy Allen.

Commander Bly's gear includes polarised macrobinoculars that filter out glare.

# DOWNFALL OF THE JEDI

"Execute Order 66."

DARTH SIDIOUS

## JUST FOLLOWING ORDERS

The bioengineered clones feel no emotion when they receive the order, and carry it out without malice. That lack of emotion prevents Jedi such as Ki-Adi-Mundi from sensing their troops' intentions through the Force.

## JEDI SURVIVORS

A few Jedi sense the danger – or get lucky. Obi-Wan evades death on Utapau, while Yoda escapes a Kashyyyk ambush with help from the Wookiees.

### VEHICLES

BARC Speeder

AT-RT

Aayla and her troops hunt Separatists through the planet Felucia's brilliantly coloured jungles.

### LOCATIONS

Felucia

Mygeeto

Cato Neimoidia

Saleucami

### NOTABLE CHARACTER

Stass Allie

**SIDIOUS SENDS ANAKIN** to Coruscant's Jedi Temple with ruthless orders: kill all the Jedi. He tells Anakin that destroying the remaining Jedi will make him strong enough with the dark side to save Padmé. Blind to everything but his terror of losing his wife, the new Sith apprentice does not question this horrifying command. Lord Vader leads clone troopers to the Jedi Temple and massacres his former friends and colleagues in the Jedi Order. Soon flames climb into the skies above Coruscant.

### SITH WITHOUT PITY
A few younglings hide in the Jedi Council Chamber, but Anakin finds them and strikes them down. His journey to the dark side is complete.

**NOTABLE CHARACTERS**

Zett Jukassa

Sors Bandeam

**VEHICLE**

XJ-2 Airspeeder

# TEMPLE ATTACK

*"Do what must be done, Lord Vader. Do not hesitate. Show no mercy."*
DARTH SIDIOUS

The clones walk beneath pylons decorated with sculptures of the Temple's four founders.

**III** REVENGE OF THE SITH

**WORRIED WITNESS**
From her apartment, Padmé sees the smoke and hears Anakin has gone to the Jedi Temple. She stays at her window, sick with worry – but with no idea what has actually happened to the man she loves.

**"TIME FOR YOU TO LEAVE, SIR"**
Bail Organa, the senator from Alderaan, visits the Jedi Temple and is stopped by clones, who blast a fugitive Padawan as Organa watches in horror. Barely escaping with his own life, Organa fears what awaits the galaxy.

**ONE TOUGH JEDI**
- After changing his mind about Grievous killing the cunning Jedi Shaak Ti early in Episode III, Lucas shot new footage in which Anakin struck her down during the Jedi Temple attack. But this scene was also cut before the film's release.

Anakin's troopers are part of the 501st Legion, later known as Vader's Fist.

**ANAKIN RETURNS** to Padmé's apartment before leaving for the Mustafar system to eliminate the Separatist leaders. Meanwhile, Bail Organa rescues Obi-Wan and Yoda, who decide they must shut down a signal from the Jedi Temple telling the Jedi to return to Coruscant. At a special session of the Galactic Senate, Palpatine – disfigured by Force lightning – celebrates the end of the Clone Wars and the failure of the Jedi rebellion. The Republic will become the Galactic Empire, and he will be its Emperor.

### FATEFUL FAREWELL

Anakin tells Padmé that the Jedi tried to overthrow the Republic, but he remains loyal to Palpatine. He tells her to have faith – he will soon return from Mustafar, and then things will be different.

**NOTABLE CHARACTER**

Sly Moore

**VEHICLE**

*Sundered Heart*

As speaker, Mas Amedda uses this staff while presiding over sessions of the Senate.

# DECLARATION OF EMPIRE

### JEDI FUGITIVES
Rescued by Senator Organa, Yoda and Obi-Wan decide to return with him to Coruscant, despite the danger to any Jedi survivors of Order 66.

### OBI-WAN'S WARNING
After witnessing Palpatine name himself Emperor, Padmé meets secretly with Obi-Wan, who tells her of Anakin's fall and asks where he has gone. Fearing for her husband's life, Padmé refuses to say.

With the Jedi destroyed, Sidious no longer fears showing his true face as a Sith Lord.

### STITCH IN TIME
- After this scene wrapped, Ian McDiarmid jumped ahead two decades (in film time) to shoot replacement footage for the DVD of Episode V in which the Emperor and Darth Vader plot to turn Luke to the dark side.

## "So this is how liberty dies – with thunderous applause."
**PADMÉ AMIDALA**

**ON MUSTAFAR, ANAKIN** slaughters the Separatist leaders, taking particular pleasure in the death of Padmé's old enemy Nute Gunray. To his surprise, Padmé's ship lands on Mustafar. She begs him to run away with her and raise their child, but Anakin says they don't have to hide: he has brought peace to the Republic, and now he and Padmé can overthrow Sidious and rule the galaxy together. He is disappointed when a horrified Padmé breaks down in tears – and his disappointment turns to rage at the sight of Obi-Wan Kenobi.

### VADER'S VISION
Padmé and C-3PO pilot her star skiff to Mustafar, unaware that Obi-Wan is hiding aboard the ship. Padmé hopes to turn Anakin away from his dark path, but finds he now dreams of conquest.

### SECRET STAGE
- Only essential members of the film crew were allowed on set for this pivotal scene, but the security was unnecessary: noisy wind machines made it impossible to hear most of the actors' lines.

# ANAKIN'S CHOICE

Consumed by the dark side, Anakin's desire to save Padmé has turned into a lust for power.

**III** REVENGE OF THE SITH

## THE STOWAWAY
When Anakin spots Obi-Wan, he thinks Padmé has turned against him, and has brought his former Master to Mustafar to kill him.

## DARK LORD'S FURY
A furious Anakin uses the Force to strangle Padmé, accusing Obi-Wan of turning her against him. Obi-Wan tries to reason with his former Padawan, but it is too late – the dark side has blinded him.

> ## "Only a Sith deals in absolutes."
> OBI-WAN KENOBI

Obi-Wan reluctantly agreed to confront Anakin after Yoda pointed out that he was not strong enough to face Sidious.

### LOCATIONS

Mustafar

Mining Complex

### NOTABLE CHARACTERS

Passel Argente

Shu Mai

### CREATURE

Mustafar Lava Flea

### VEHICLE

Naboo Star Skiff

**WHILE OBI-WAN** searches for Anakin, Yoda takes on the Sith apprentice's Master, battling Sidious in his office beneath the Senate chamber. The Sith Lord relishes the chance to destroy the legendary Jedi, and uses the dark side of the Force to hurl Senate pods at Yoda. The two opponents are among the most powerful Force-users in the galaxy, but the ascendant dark side has made Sidious stronger. Yoda realises he cannot defeat the new Emperor, and can hope only to escape from him.

### BENEATH THE SENATE

As Yoda duels with Sidious, the Emperor taunts him, predicting that Darth Vader will become more powerful than either of them.

## CORUSCANT SHOWDOWN

Even the most powerful Jedi has limits, and the fight with Sidious exhausts Yoda.

III REVENGE OF THE SITH

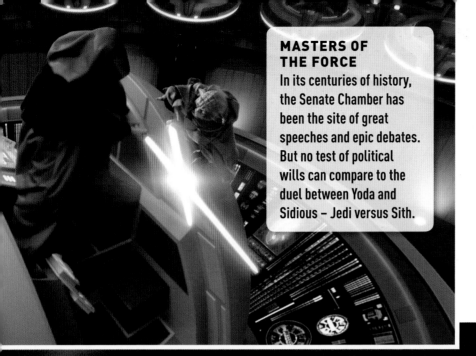

### MASTERS OF THE FORCE
In its centuries of history, the Senate Chamber has been the site of great speeches and epic debates. But no test of political wills can compare to the duel between Yoda and Sidious – Jedi versus Sith.

### THE SEARCH BEGINS
Yoda loses his grip and falls into the depths of the Senate Chamber, but Sidious's clone troopers can find no trace of him. The Jedi Master has fled, escaping the Senate in Bail Organa's speeder.

### HELPING HAND
- Lucas's old friend and Indiana Jones co-creator Steven Spielberg directed early computer animatics of the Senate duel, which featured the fight being watched by audiences across the galaxy.

## "If so powerful you are, why leave?"
YODA

Sidious draws on the dark side to create Force lightning of great power.

### LOCATION

Palpatine's Senate Office

**OBI-WAN FINDS ANAKIN** and they begin to duel, battling with their lightsabers and the power of the Force. The furious fight damages the protective fields shielding the mining complex from the heat of Mustafar's lava, and the two combatants continue their fight along a blazing river of fire, trading blows from atop a mining platform and a confused droid. Obi-Wan leaps from the fiery river to the bank, gaining the high ground. Filled with dark-side rage, Anakin attacks anyway. It is a grave mistake.

## BROTHER AGAINST BROTHER

Anakin and Obi-Wan use everything from lightsabers to fists as they try to defeat each other. Convinced the Jedi have betrayed both him and the Republic, Anakin seeks to kill his former Master and friend.

# DUEL ON MUSTAFAR

**DROID**

Mustafar Droid

Obi-Wan learned to use the Force for knowledge and defence, not to attack. But he has no choice against Anakin.

### THE HIGH GROUND
Obi-Wan escapes the dangers of the lava river first, leaping to a high bank. Still feeling compassion for his old Padawan, he warns Anakin against a risky attack. Anakin is too full of pain and fury to listen.

### FATE OF THE JEDI
Anakin's attack leaves him maimed and helpless. Obi-Wan turns away in grief and horror as fire begins to consume the Jedi's Chosen One.

Lava erupts from Mustafar's rivers, damaging the unshielded mining equipment.

## "You were my brother, Anakin! I loved you!"
### OBI-WAN KENOBI

### COOL FOR CATS
- A visual effects crew spent months shooting these scenes using a 6 m by 9 m (20 ft by 30 ft) model of Mustafar. The lava was actually cool – it was made from Methocel, a powder that becomes a gel when mixed with cold water. Cat litter was added to form clumps and lights below the model made the lava appear orange.

**LEAVING MUSTAFAR**, Obi-Wan takes Padmé to the planet Polis Massa, where Yoda and Bail Organa are waiting. Medical droids try to save her life, but their efforts are in vain – she has lost the will to live. The droids deliver not one baby but twins, and the dying Padmé names them Luke and Leia. Yoda, Obi-Wan and Bail Organa know Anakin Skywalker's children will be strong with the Force. They must find a way to prevent them from being found by the evil agents of the new Sith Emperor.

### DROID DOCTORS
The lonely world of Polis Massa is a good place for births that must be kept secret. The facility's droids do not understand their failure to save Padmé, but Bail Organa does: some broken hearts cannot be mended.

# THE BIRTH OF THE TWINS

### NOTABLE CHARACTERS

Queen Apailana

Sio Bibble

Ruwee Naberrie

Jobal Naberrie

Sola Naberrie

### LOCATION

Polis Massa

*"Obi-Wan, there is good in him. I know there is."*
PADMÉ AMIDALA

### EARLY DEBUT
- For close-ups, both Luke and Leia were played by Aidan Barton, the son of film editor Roger Barton. A carefully wrapped rubber baby was used for other shots of the twins.

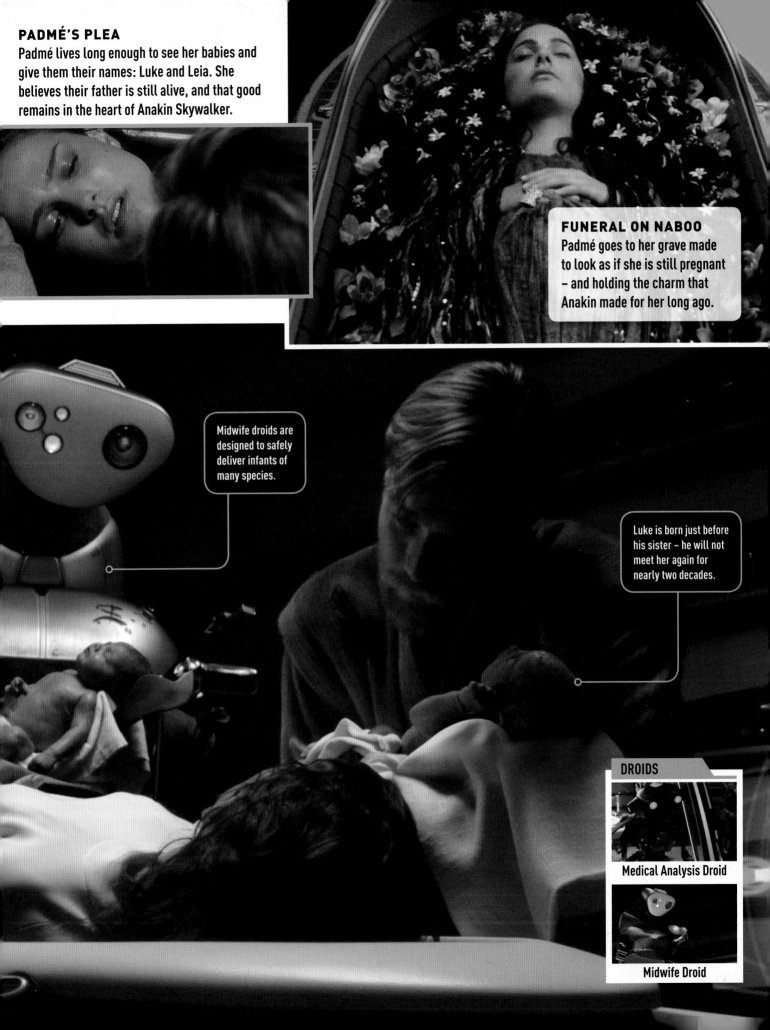

## PADMÉ'S PLEA
Padmé lives long enough to see her babies and give them their names: Luke and Leia. She believes their father is still alive, and that good remains in the heart of Anakin Skywalker.

## FUNERAL ON NABOO
Padmé goes to her grave made to look as if she is still pregnant – and holding the charm that Anakin made for her long ago.

Midwife droids are designed to safely deliver infants of many species.

Luke is born just before his sister – he will not meet her again for nearly two decades.

DROIDS

Medical Analysis Droid

Midwife Droid

**THINKING ANAKIN** is mortally wounded, a grieving Obi-Wan took his old friend's lightsaber and left him on the lava bank. He and the surviving Jedi believe the Chosen One is dead, another victim of the Sith. But the Emperor senses Anakin's peril, and finds him still alive by the burning river. Medical droids treat his injuries, and he is encased in black armour that will preserve his ruined body. Trapped behind a dark mask, Darth Vader finds the past too painful to recall, and begins to forget his former self.

## SITH MERCY

Anakin's injuries leave him more machine than man – he will never be the powerful apprentice that Sidious hoped for. But the Sith Lord can make use of Vader while waiting for a worthy replacement.

# THE RISE OF DARTH VADER

Binders keep Anakin from damaging the medical equipment during his painful transformation.

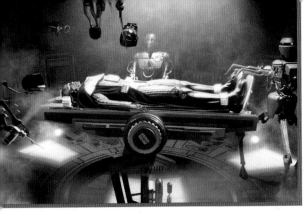

## GRIM TRANSFORMATION

Sidious takes Anakin to Coruscant, where his life is saved but his humanity is all but lost. Those who oppose Emperor Palpatine's rule will soon fear the name of Darth Vader, his mightiest servant.

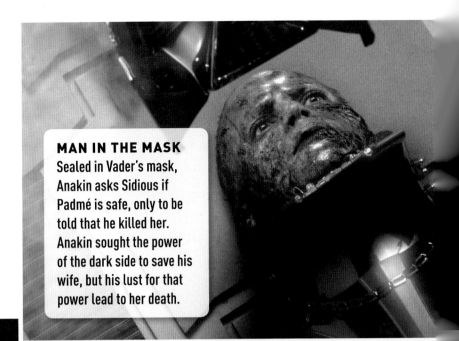

### MAN IN THE MASK

Sealed in Vader's mask, Anakin asks Sidious if Padmé is safe, only to be told that he killed her. Anakin sought the power of the dark side to save his wife, but his lust for that power lead to her death.

Seeker droids spy on Sidious's enemies and record episodes of interest for Sith meditation.

### MOVIE MONSTER

- Vader's transformation and his struggle to break his chains recall the creation of the monster played by Boris Karloff in the 1931 horror film classic *Frankenstein*.

## "Lord Vader, can you hear me?"

### DARTH SIDIOUS

**NOTABLE CHARACTER**

Darth Vader

**LOCATION**

Rehabilitation Centre

**VEHICLES**

*Theta*-class Shuttle

V-wing Fighter

**DROIDS**

2-1B Droid

Chopper Droid

**THE CHILDEN OF** Anakin and Padmé are split up for their safety. Obi-Wan takes Luke to the Tatooine moisture farm owned by Anakin's stepbrother, Owen Lars, while Bail Organa says he and his wife will raise Leia as their daughter on Alderaan. Organa vows to oppose the Emperor in the Senate, but Yoda and Obi-Wan are forced to go into exile, hiding from the Emperor's servants and seeking to strengthen their connection to the Force. The Jedi are defeated, but one day Anakin's children may help the Order to rise again.

### THE EMPEROR'S WILL
Darth Vader joins his Master in stamping out resistance to the new Empire, watching over projects such as the construction of the Death Star.

# EXILES AND HOPES

### ALL TOGETHER NOW
- Joel Edgerton (Owen) was unavailable for filming and shot separately from Ewan McGregor and Bonnie Piesse (Beru). He was added digitally at a later date.

- Appropriately, this scene was McGregor's last during principal photography.

Vaporators extract up to 1.5 litres (3 pints) of water per day from Tatooine's dry air.

 REVENGE OF THE SITH

## PRINCESS OF ALDERAAN
Bail Organa begins the long struggle to restore freedom to the galaxy – a cause that his adopted daughter will one day join, following the lead of her birth mother Padmé Amidala.

## SON OF THE SUNS
Owen and his wife, Beru, take Luke from Obi-Wan, hoping the boy will grow up safe on Tatooine – and unaware of his father's tragic fate. But the will of the Force has other plans for the son of Anakin Skywalker.

### LOCATION
Dagobah

### NOTABLE CHARACTERS
Luke Skywalker

Leia Organa

Breha Organa

Captain Antilles

At first Owen is glad Obi-Wan is nearby, watching over Luke. But he comes to resent the Jedi's presence.

EIGHTEEN YEARS after the fall of the Republic, Emperor Palpatine's warships and stormtroopers have crushed resistance to his rule in much of the galaxy. His few opponents have formed the Rebel Alliance, and their spies have stolen the plans for the Death Star. This creation is an Imperial battle station with enough firepower to destroy an entire planet. The rebel spies transmit the stolen plans to Princess Leia Organa, a Senator from Alderaan and secret Rebel Alliance leader. Leia races for home – but the forces of the Empire are not far behind.

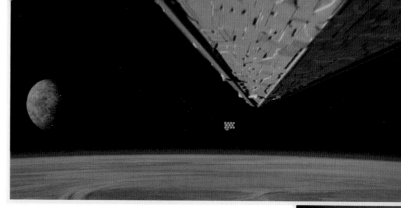

### ENCOUNTER AT TATOOINE
Above the desert planet Tatooine, an Imperial Star Destroyer cripples Leia's ship and brings it aboard. The Imperial hunters are led by Darth Vader, the Sith Lord feared as Emperor Palpatine's evil enforcer.

# A PRINCESS CAPTURED

### SWITCHING SHIPS
- The *Tantive IV* was originally Han Solo's pirate ship, but a similar design appeared in the TV show *Space: 1999*, which debuted during production. Joe Johnston created an updated model with a new "hammerhead" cockpit, and that design became Leia's ship.

The Republic's clones have been replaced by recruits trained for blind loyalty to the Empire.

The *Tantive IV*'s troopers are brave, but no match for veteran Imperial troops in armour.

IV  A NEW HOPE

## DESPERATE MISSION

Leia hides the Death Star plans in the memory of the astromech droid R2-D2, who flees her ship with his friend C-3PO in an escape pod. Then she is captured by prowling stormtroopers, who bring her to Vader.

### DEFYING THE SENATE

An angry Leia objects that she is a senator on a diplomatic mission, but Vader growls that she is part of the Rebel Alliance and a traitor.

### VEHICLES

Imperial Star Destroyer     *Tantive IV*     Escape Pod

### NOTABLE CHARACTERS

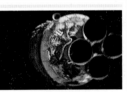

Princess Leia Organa     Commander Jir

## "There'll be no escape for the princess this time."

C-3PO

**BEFORE HER CAPTURE** Princess Leia ordered R2-D2 to take the Death Star plans to Obi-Wan Kenobi, the fugitive Jedi Knight who served her father, Bail Organa, in the Clone Wars. She recorded a message begging him to deliver the droid to Bail on Alderaan. The droids land on Tatooine in an escape pod, but quarrel over what to do next. C-3PO's memory was erased long ago and he has no recall of the years he spent on Tatooine. The protocol droid only knows he has had quite enough adventures.

**SEPARATE WAYS**
R2-D2 insists he knows which way to go on Tatooine, but C-3PO disagrees and trudges off across the desert world's tawny dunes.

## THE SANDS OF TATOOINE

**DROIDS**

Power Droid

RA-7 Protocol Droid

CZ-series Secretary Droid

**CREATURE**

Dewback

**VEHICLES**

Sandcrawler

Imperial Landing Craft

**"We're doomed!"**

C-3PO

The Jawas hit R2-D2 with a burst from a homemade ion blaster, leaving his circuits briefly overloaded.

IV   A NEW HOPE

## DROID HUNT

In orbit, Darth Vader hears about the escape pod and concludes Leia hid the plans inside. A squad of stormtroopers finds the pod and a bit of plating in the sand. Now they know to look for droids.

## JAWA CAPTIVES

Jawa scavengers ambush R2-D2 in a canyon and take him to their sandcrawler, intending to sell him to Tatooine's settlers. The rusty vehicle is full of droids, including another captive – C-3PO.

Jawa bands use sandcrawlers as transports, droid repair shops and mobile fortresses.

## INVASION FORCE?

■ Scenes with the Jawa sandcrawler were shot near the border of Tunisia and Libya. Worried Libyan officials looked over the vehicle to make sure it was not part of a Tunisian military operation.

**THE JAWAS SELL** the droids to Owen Lars and his nephew Luke Skywalker. Luke is a gifted pilot who dreams of going to the Imperial academy, and is frustrated that he is stuck on his uncle's moisture farm. While cleaning R2-D2, Luke finds a partial message from a mysterious young woman, pleading for help from someone named Obi-Wan Kenobi. R2-D2 is determined to complete his mission, and tricks Luke into removing the restraining bolt that prevents the droid from leaving the farm.

## MAKING A PURCHASE

Droids are common in the galaxy, so Owen Lars does not remember C-3PO from his younger days. He buys the protocol droid and another named R5-D4, who malfunctions and is replaced by R2-D2.

## MEET LUKE SKYWALKER

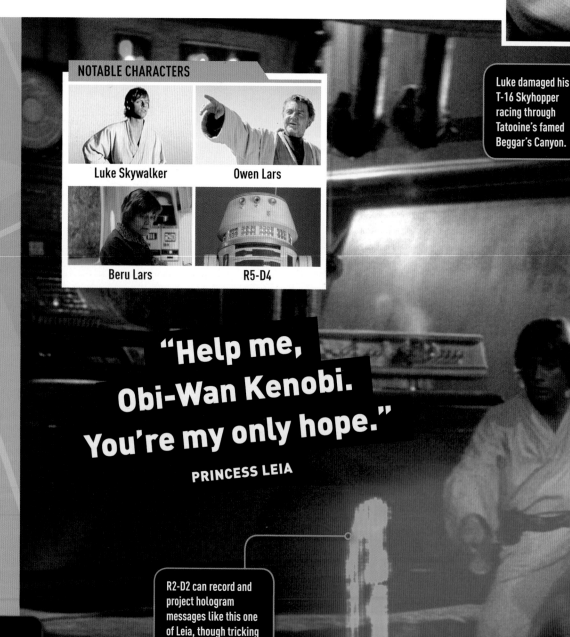

### NOTABLE CHARACTERS

Luke Skywalker

Owen Lars

Beru Lars

R5-D4

Luke damaged his T-16 Skyhopper racing through Tatooine's famed Beggar's Canyon.

## "Help me, Obi-Wan Kenobi. You're my only hope."

PRINCESS LEIA

R2-D2 can record and project hologram messages like this one of Leia, though tricking Luke is not exactly standard programming.

**IV** | A NEW HOPE

## A FAMILIAR ARGUMENT
Owen argues with Luke about going to the academy, and Beru says Luke has too much of his father in him. Owen replies, "That's what I'm afraid of."

## RUNAWAY ROBOT
Luke discovers that R2-D2 has vanished into the night. The threat of Tusken Raiders makes it too dangerous to search for him now, so Luke decides to hunt for R2 in the morning, before Uncle Owen learns he has gone.

### DROIDS

KPR Servant Droid

R1-series Astromech

WED Droid

### IDENTITY CRISIS
- When the filming in Tunisia was complete, Lucas told actor Mark Hamill that his character's name had been changed from Luke Starkiller to Luke Skywalker. The name Starkiller was revived in 2008 for the *Star Wars: The Force Unleashed* video game.

**LUKE FINDS R2-D2** in the Jundland Wastes, but Tusken Raiders find Luke. He is saved by Obi-Wan Kenobi, who says he was once a Jedi Knight like Luke's father. Obi-Wan has been saving his father's lightsaber to give to Luke one day. Stunned by this revelation, Luke asks how his father died. Obi-Wan hesitates, then says he was betrayed and murdered by Darth Vader. R2-D2 plays Princess Leia's message, in which she begs Obi-Wan to take the droid and the Death Star plans to her father, Bail Organa, on Alderaan in hopes that the battle station can be stopped.

## TUSKEN ATTACK

A band of Tusken Raiders attacks Luke, knocking him unconscious and causing C-3PO to stumble off a bluff. But the savage nomads flee at the sound of a krayt dragon, Tatooine's deadliest predator.

# A DESTINY REVEALED

**CREATURE**

Bantha

**VEHICLE**

Landspeeder

**NOTABLE CHARACTER**

Obi-Wan Kenobi

After Luke repairs C-3PO's left arm, the droid shuts down his external systems, allowing the circuits to reknit.

Luke was told by his Uncle Owen that his father was a navigator on a spice freighter.

## "This is the weapon of a Jedi Knight."

OBI-WAN KENOBI

**IV** A NEW HOPE

## LUKE'S GUARDIAN
The call of a krayt dragon is a trick of Obi-Wan's. The Jedi exile has watched over Luke since infancy, waiting for the son of Anakin Skywalker to grow old enough to learn the truth about his past and fulfill his destiny.

## THE WILL OF THE FORCE
When R2-D2 plays Leia's message, Obi-Wan realises the will of the Force is in motion – and it is time for his long exile on Tatooine to end.

## SCARY STUNT
■ Mark Hamill's look of fear when attacked by the Tusken Raider is all too real – stuntman Peter Diamond could not see through his mask, and it was up to Hamill to dodge the blows.

OBI-WAN TELLS LUKE he must learn the ways of the Force if he is to come with him to Alderaan. Luke has dreamed of such an adventure, but now he hesitates – his aunt and uncle need him. He agrees to take Obi-Wan as far as the town of Anchorhead. But fate has other plans for Luke: he and Obi-Wan discover the Jawas' sandcrawler, blasted apart by stormtroopers. Luke wonders why the Empire would slaughter Jawas, then realises they were actually hunting the droids. Now his aunt and uncle are in terrible danger.

### GRIM DISCOVERY
Bantha tracks and shattered axes suggest the Tuskens destroyed the sandcrawler, but Obi-Wan knows better. This is the Empire's work.

# VICTIMS OF THE EMPIRE

> "I want to learn the ways of the Force and become a Jedi like my father."
>
> LUKE SKYWALKER

### WESTERN HOMAGE
- This sequence mirrors one in John Ford's 1956 classic *The Searchers*, in which Comanche raiders burn the Edwards' farm after luring away the men with a diversion.

## MURDER ON TATOOINE

Luke races back to the farm, but it is too late: stormtroopers have killed his aunt and uncle, and the only life Luke has ever known is gone. Luke's grief turns to determination.

## A NEW PATH

Luke returns to Obi-Wan and asks to go with the Jedi Knight to Alderaan, and follow his father's path. This journey will draw Luke into the ancient conflict between Jedi and Sith.

Cliegg Lars built this entry dome leading down to the farm's central well.

A horrified Luke spots the bodies of his aunt and uncle, slain by the stormtroopers when they tried to flee their home.

**OBI-WAN AND LUKE** travel to the sleazy spaceport of Mos Eisley in search of a pilot who can take them to Alderaan. Their search leads them to a cantina filled with alien villains and bullies. When two thugs menace Luke, Obi-Wan cuts them down with his lightsaber. Obi-Wan hires a smooth-talking Corellian smuggler named Han Solo as his pilot, along with his first mate, Chewbacca the Wookiee. But the Empire's spies are still hunting the droids, stormtroopers are closing in and Star Destroyers await any ship that tries to escape from Tatooine.

### JEDI MIND TRICK
Stormtroopers stop Luke's speeder and demand to know about the droids. Obi-Wan uses the Force to cloud the troopers' minds so they can pass.

**DROID**

Mark IV Sentry Droid

**VEHICLE**

*Millennium Falcon*

Chewbacca keeps ammunition for his favourite weapon, a bowcaster, in a bandolier across his shaggy chest.

# HIVE OF SCUM AND VILLAINY

"Watch yourself – this place can be a little rough."

OBI-WAN KENOBI

**LOCATIONS**

Mos Eisley

Cantina

**IV** A NEW HOPE

## PILOTS FOR HIRE
Starship pilots of all species frequent the cantina, where they shelter from the heat and wait for work – not all of which is legal. As Obi-Wan warns Luke, the place can be a little rough.

## SUDDEN DEPARTURE
Han Solo agrees to take Luke, Obi-Wan and the droids to Alderaan aboard his ship, the *Millennium Falcon*. He exchanges fire with a squad of stormtroopers and blasts out of Mos Eisley, racing past the Star Destroyers into hyperspace.

The cantina's alcoves are prized spots because no one can sneak up without being seen.

## NOTABLE CHARACTERS

Han Solo

Greedo

Ponda Baba

Doctor Evazan

Garindan

## ORIGINAL GANGSTER
- George Lucas shot a scene in which Jabba the Hutt confronts Han, but a tight budget forced him to portray Jabba as a portly human, and the scene was cut from the film. A sluglike Jabba was digitally added for 1998's special edition, along with a cameo by Boba Fett.

**THE DEATH STAR** is nearly complete after years of secret construction. Its commander is Grand Moff Tarkin, a ruthless and ambitious Imperial governor who believes a demonstration of the Death Star's destructive power will end all opposition to Imperial rule. Tarkin's ideal target for such a show of force is the rebels' hidden base. But when Leia refuses to reveal its location, Tarkin has an idea for another target. He will destroy Alderaan, home to Princess Leia and millions of others.

## PALPATINE'S PROCLAMATION

Tarkin tells his henchmen that Emperor Palpatine has dissolved the Senate, the last remnant of the Republic. Governors such as Tarkin now control the galaxy, and fear of the Death Star will keep its star systems in line.

# THE DEATH OF ALDERAAN

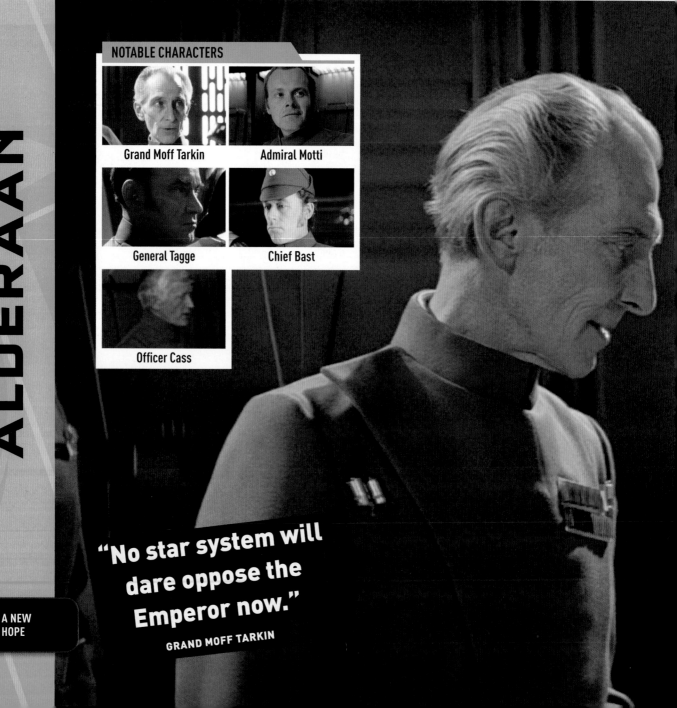

### NOTABLE CHARACTERS

Grand Moff Tarkin

Admiral Motti

General Tagge

Chief Bast

Officer Cass

> "No star system will dare oppose the Emperor now."
>
> GRAND MOFF TARKIN

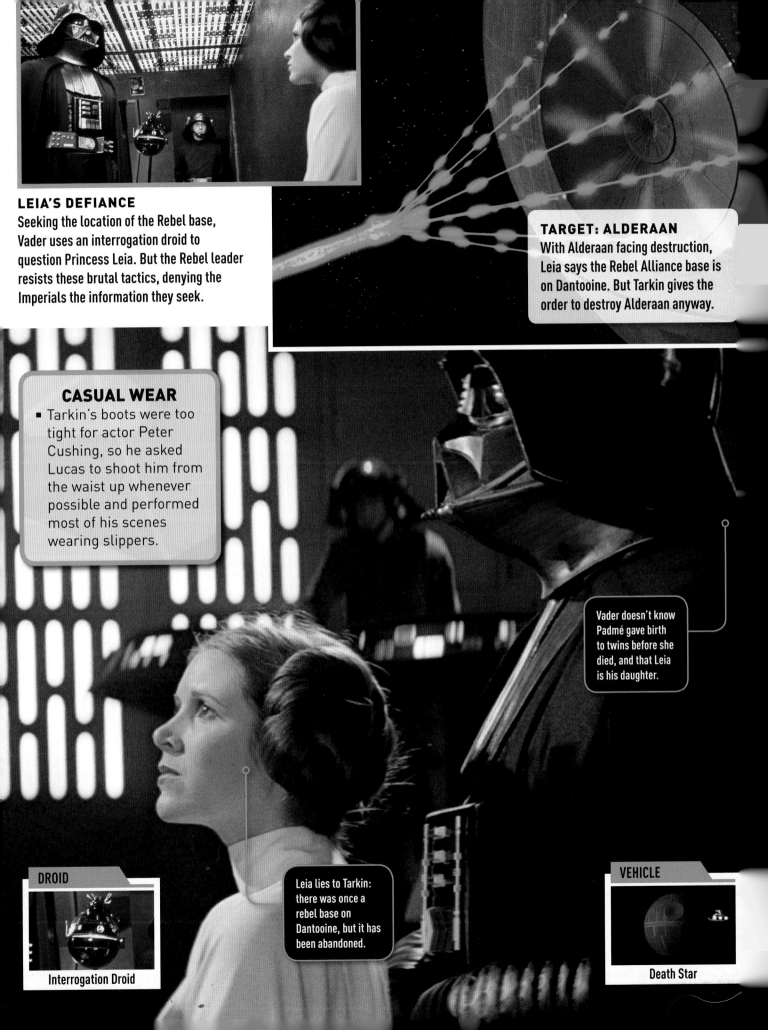

## LEIA'S DEFIANCE

Seeking the location of the Rebel base, Vader uses an interrogation droid to question Princess Leia. But the Rebel leader resists these brutal tactics, denying the Imperials the information they seek.

## TARGET: ALDERAAN

With Alderaan facing destruction, Leia says the Rebel Alliance base is on Dantooine. But Tarkin gives the order to destroy Alderaan anyway.

## CASUAL WEAR

- Tarkin's boots were too tight for actor Peter Cushing, so he asked Lucas to shoot him from the waist up whenever possible and performed most of his scenes wearing slippers.

Vader doesn't know Padmé gave birth to twins before she died, and that Leia is his daughter.

**DROID**

Interrogation Droid

Leia lies to Tarkin: there was once a rebel base on Dantooine, but it has been abandoned.

**VEHICLE**

Death Star

**THE _FALCON_ EMERGES** from hyperspace and has to avoid a storm of debris. Surprised, Han tells his passengers that his position is correct, but Alderaan has been destroyed. After a TIE fighter buzzes the _Falcon_, Han gives chase, trying to catch the Imperial craft before it reaches a small moon hanging ahead of them in deep space. Obi-Wan is the first to realise their mistake: the small moon is actually the Death Star. Han and Chewie try to turn their ship around, but it is too late – the _Falcon_ is caught in a powerful tractor beam.

## FORCED TO SHUT DOWN
Han watches in dismay as his easy charter turns into a nightmare: the Death Star's tractor beam drags the _Falcon_ aboard.

# THE FALCON CAPTURED

**VEHICLE**

TIE Fighter

To mislead the Empire, Han launches several escape pods before the _Falcon_ is captured.

## CHANGE OF SCENERY
- Only two-thirds of the _Millennium Falcon_ were built, but the ship was still too big to move. The crew left the pirate ship in place, tearing down the Mos Eisley docking bay set and replacing it with the Death Star hangar.

- Other actors considered for the part of Luke Skywalker were Robby Benson, William Katt and Andrew Stevens.

With the _Falcon_ not secured, more stormtroopers arrive from lower levels via a cargo lift.

### RIPPLES IN THE FORCE

Vader's troops inspect the *Falcon* and find her empty of both living beings and droids. Sensing an odd stirring in the Force, the Sith Lord orders a thorough scan of every part of the dingy freighter.

### SMUGGLED GOODS

Han and his passengers are hidden in the secret compartments he and Chewie use for smuggling. They ambush a pair of stormtroopers sent aboard the ship and take over a nearby control room.

> ## "That's no moon. It's a space station."
> #### OBI-WAN KENOBI

### NOTABLE CHARACTERS

Captain Khurgee

Lieutenant Treidum

**R2-D2 TAPS** into the Death Star's network, showing Obi-Wan the location of the controls for the tractor beam. The old Jedi tells Luke to look after the droids and departs. But R2 discovers something else: Princess Leia has been taken prisoner, and is scheduled for termination. Luke convinces Han to try a rescue mission and they disguise themselves as stormtroopers, with Chewie as their prisoner. When the guards on the prison level doubt their story, the three must blast their way out of trouble. With more stormtroopers on the way, Luke runs to find the captive princess.

## A DIFFERENT PATH

Luke is disappointed when Obi-Wan tells him to remain behind. The Jedi will rely on the Force to move undetected, and reassures Luke that, "Your destiny lies along a different path than mine."

## CANINE CO-PILOT

- Lucas's idea for Chewie began with his dog Indiana, who liked to ride in the passenger seat of his car. For Chewie's growls, Ben Burtt combined sounds made by a walrus named Petulia and a cinnamon bear named Pooh.

**HEROES IN DISGUISE**

### REWARDING RESCUE?
Han refuses to risk his life on a dangerous rescue mission, but reconsiders when Luke promises that he will earn a big reward.

### COMPANY'S COMING
The firefight in the detention block raises alarms all over the Death Star, and no amount of fast talking from Han can convince the Imperials that all is well. Han, Chewie and Luke are about to have company.

## "Where are you taking this...thing?"
LIEUTENANT CHILDSEN

**NOTABLE CHARACTER**

Lieutenant Childsen

**DROID**

Mouse Droid

Han uses a DLT-19 blaster rifle in his guise as Chewbacca's Imperial captor.

Luke unlocks Chewbacca's binders once they're in the lift and headed for the prison level.

**LUKE FREES LEIA,** who is not impressed until he says he is with Obi-Wan and has her missing droid. The rescue attempt soon becomes a disaster, as stormtroopers trap the four inside the cell bay. Leia grabs Luke's gun and blasts open a grate leading to a garbage unit below the detention block. But the garbage masher is no escape: its door is locked, the droids do not respond to Luke's calls for help and something hungry lurks within the muck. Bad enough – and then the walls start to close in…

### PRISONER OF THE EMPIRE
Luke saves Leia from her cell, but he and his friends are trapped on the prison level by stormtroopers. The princess soon decides that she will have to save herself.

**CREATURE**

**Dianoga**

The hatch leading out of unit 3263827 is magnetically sealed to prevent leaks.

Garbage mashers compact scrap and waste, which is then jettisoned into space.

**IV**

A NEW HOPE

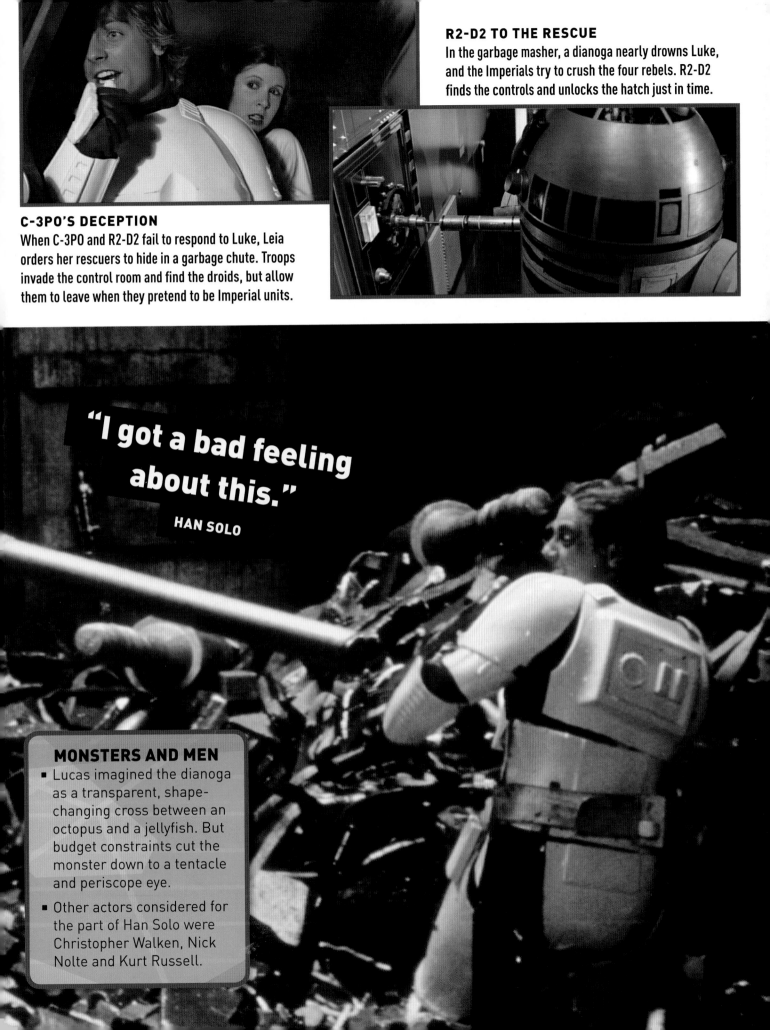

### R2-D2 TO THE RESCUE
In the garbage masher, a dianoga nearly drowns Luke, and the Imperials try to crush the four rebels. R2-D2 finds the controls and unlocks the hatch just in time.

### C-3PO'S DECEPTION
When C-3PO and R2-D2 fail to respond to Luke, Leia orders her rescuers to hide in a garbage chute. Troops invade the control room and find the droids, but allow them to leave when they pretend to be Imperial units.

> "I got a bad feeling about this."
> **HAN SOLO**

### MONSTERS AND MEN
- Lucas imagined the dianoga as a transparent, shape-changing cross between an octopus and a jellyfish. But budget constraints cut the monster down to a tentacle and periscope eye.
- Other actors considered for the part of Han Solo were Christopher Walken, Nick Nolte and Kurt Russell.

**OBI-WAN EVADES** squads of soldiers and deactivates the tractor beam, but the Death Star is now on high alert. Imperial troops chase the rebels, forcing them to split into two groups and fight running battles with their pursuers. Han and Chewie feel like half the station is after them, but Luke and Leia are in worse trouble: they wind up trapped on the edge of a chasm, with stormtroopers ahead of them, stormtroopers behind them and no way to get across the bridge to safety.

### A JEDI ALONE
Obi-Wan shuts down the tractor beam without being seen, but Vader senses his presence and is determined to confront him.

## SWING TO FREEDOM

### COMPETITION AND TRADITION

- A stormtrooper shot in this scene lets out a yell first heard in the 1951 movie *Distant Drums*. Ben Burtt called the sound the "Wilhelm scream", and it has become a movie staple, used in all six *Star Wars* films and more than 200 other motion pictures.

- Lucas also considered actresses Jodie Foster, Terri Nunn and Amy Irving for the part of Princess Leia.

**"I think we took a wrong turn!"**
LUKE SKYWALKER

**IV** A NEW HOPE

### REBELS ON THE RUN

After escaping the garbage masher, the rebels must find their way to the docking bay holding the *Falcon*. They split up under fire, with Han yelling for Luke and Leia to return to the ship.

### NOWHERE TO RUN

Chased by stormtroopers, Luke and Leia nearly fall into a deep trench and are marooned on a retracted bridge. Luke lassos machinery far above, grabs Leia and swings out over the void.

Luke and Leia swing across the chasm on a fibercord line and grappling hook, attached to Luke's stormtrooper utility belt.

The bridge could not be extended because Luke blasted the door controls to keep the stormtroopers from opening it.

**OBI-WAN MAKES HIS WAY** back to the *Falcon*, but a dark figure is waiting for him – Darth Vader, whom Obi-Wan left for dead nearly 20 years ago on Mustafar. Vader tells his former Master he should not have come back. But Obi-Wan has learned much during his years of exile – the Jedi warns his former pupil that striking him down will cause him to become more powerful than the Sith Lord can imagine. When Obi-Wan sees that Luke and his friends can reach the *Falcon*, he sacrifices himself to let them escape.

## ONCE BROTHERS, NOW ENEMIES

Obi-Wan has had years to regret the mistakes he made training Anakin Skywalker, the legendary Chosen One. He considers Anakin all but dead: Vader is consumed by evil and more machine than man.

# LIGHTSABER DUEL

Slowed by age, Obi-Wan is not the duellist he once was. But the Force is still his ally.

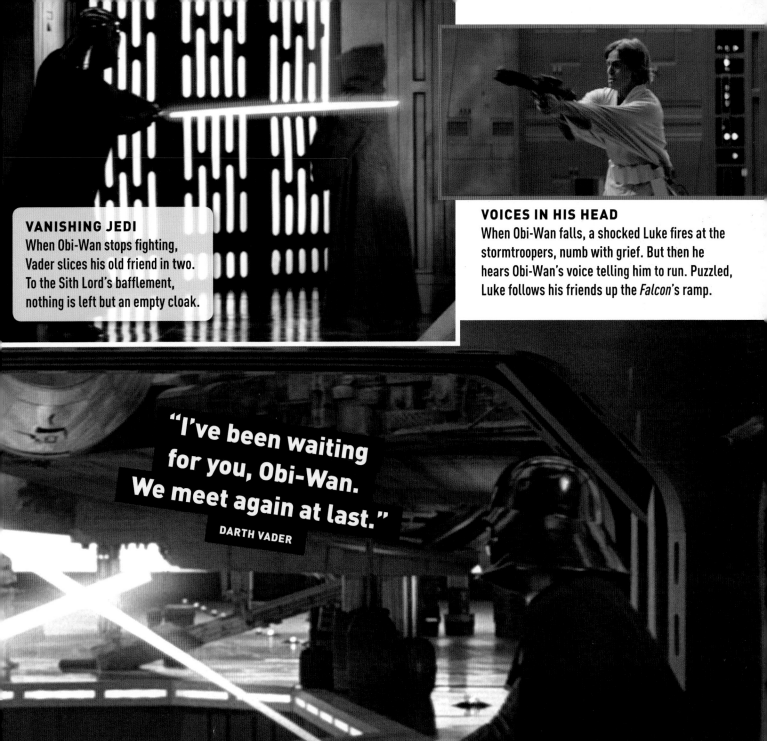

### VANISHING JEDI
When Obi-Wan stops fighting, Vader slices his old friend in two. To the Sith Lord's bafflement, nothing is left but an empty cloak.

### VOICES IN HIS HEAD
When Obi-Wan falls, a shocked Luke fires at the stormtroopers, numb with grief. But then he hears Obi-Wan's voice telling him to run. Puzzled, Luke follows his friends up the *Falcon*'s ramp.

> "I've been waiting for you, Obi-Wan. We meet again at last."
>
> DARTH VADER

### EXIT ALEC
■ Originally, Obi-Wan survived and fled aboard the *Falcon*. But the character had little to do for the rest of the film, and Lucas decided he should be killed off. Actor Alec Guinness threatened to quit over the change, but Lucas convinced him that the change was better for the overall story.

Vader's cybernetic limbs force him to rely on brute strength and the dark side in a fight.

**HAN RUNS TO** the *Falcon*'s cockpit and spins the freighter around in a dizzyingly tight turn, rocketing out of the Death Star hangar and away into space. Next the *Falcon* must get past the TIE fighters that serve as the battle station's sentry ships. Luke and Han control the freighter's guns as the Imperial fighters swarm around the battered ship. The *Falcon* escapes, but Princess Leia knows the fight is not over. She is grimly certain that the Empire allowed them to get away, and will soon follow them to the Rebel Alliance's hidden base.

### "HERE THEY COME!"
TIE fighters come at the *Falcon* from all angles, deadly laser cannons raking her shields and threatening to overwhelm her systems. Luke and Han struggle to target the small, agile fighters.

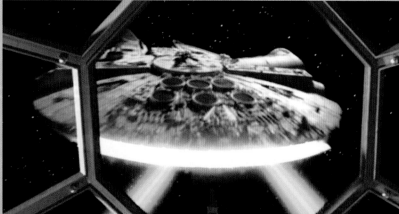

## FLIGHT OF THE FALCON

### TECHNOLOGICAL TRIUMPH
- The key to *A New Hope*'s visual effects revolution was John Dykstra's "motion-control camera". The computer-controlled camera allowed the film's visual effects wizards to create shots that were much more complex than had been seen before.

**IV**  A NEW HOPE

> ## "Great, kid! Don't get cocky!"
> **HAN SOLO**

## "SHE'S GOT IT WHERE IT COUNTS"

The *Falcon* looks dilapidated, but her battered exterior is misleading: Han's various "special modifications" give his ship the speed and firepower of a warship. The only question is: will the rest of her hold together?

## NEXT STOP: YAVIN

Luke and Han destroy the fighters, and Leia and Chewie celebrate their escape. However, the Death Star is tracking them through hyperspace.

Lando Calrissian installed the *Falcon*'s top laser cannon, while Han added another to protect her belly.

The *Falcon*'s targeting computers automatically adjust for the fighters' speed and likely course.

AT THE HIDDEN base on Yavin 4, technicians analyse the Death Star plans and find a weakness: a small exhaust port leading to the station's main reactor. The Rebel Alliance prepares a desperate attack plan: X-wing fighters will slip through the Death Star's defences, evade its surface guns and use precise targeting computers to take a million-to-one shot. Luke joins the attack, flying with R2-D2, but Han refuses. Solo thinks attacking the Empire's battle station is suicidal, not courageous.

**TARGETING THE DEATH STAR**
Rebel pilots fear the mission to destroy the Death Star is impossible, but the Alliance has no alternative. The Empire must be stopped.

# THEIR MOST DESPERATE HOUR

**NOTABLE CHARACTERS**

General Dodonna

Wedge Antilles (Red 2)

Biggs Darklighter (Red 3)

Garven Dreis (Red Leader)

Dutch Vander (Gold Leader)

Commander Willard

**LOCATIONS**

Yavin

Yavin 4

Great Temple of Massassi

"Look at the size of that thing!"

WEDGE ANTILLES

X-wings are powerful fighters, but Luke knows they handle much like his beloved T-16 Skyhopper.

IV A NEW HOPE

## LOOKING OUT FOR NUMBER ONE

Han gets his reward for saving Princess Leia and makes preparations to leave. Luke is dismayed, and Chewie is disappointed – he wants to fight. But Han insists he knows what he is doing.

## GALACTIC SHOWDOWN

Rebel pilots in their X-wings and Y-wings are astonished at the size of the Death Star, but keep their cool as they line up in attack formation. The fight to restore freedom to the galaxy has begun!

## VEHICLES

X-wing Fighter

Y-wing Fighter

Luke flies as Red 5 at Yavin. Biggs, his childhood friend from Tatooine, is Red 3.

## SEEING RED

- Luke's original call sign was Blue 5. But blue markings would have disappeared against the bluescreen used for filming scenes that would include visual effects. So Luke and his fellow pilots had to become Red Squadron.

## X-WINGS AND TIE FIGHTERS

battle above the Death Star, jockeying for position as laserfire blasts out from the gun towers below. Vader joins the battle and destroys a squad of Y-wings before they can reach the exhaust port. Red Leader reaches the target and launches a proton torpedo, but the shot misses and in the narrow trench he and his wingmen are easy targets for Vader. The Alliance is running out of pilots, as the Death Star draws ever nearer. Luke Skywalker is the rebels' last hope.

### UNEXPECTED STRATEGY
The Death Star's designers imagined having to fight off big warships, not tiny starfighters. The station's turbolasers cannot track the X-wings, forcing the Empire to send up its TIE fighters.

The exhaust port is ray-shielded, so the X-wings must use proton torpedoes.

> ## "Stay on target! Stay on target!"
> DAVISH "POPS" KRAIL, GOLD 5

## ATTACK THE DEATH STAR

### NOTABLE CHARACTERS

| | | |
|---|---|---|
| John D. (Red 4) | Jek Porkins (Red 6) | Theron Nett (Red 10) |
| Pops (Gold 5) | Tiree (Gold 2) | Lieutenant Tanbris |

## AN ANXIOUS VIGIL
On Yavin 4, Leia and C-3PO fret at each transmission from the battle, hoping Luke and R2-D2 stay safe – and succeed in stopping the Death Star.

## DEATH STAR DOGFIGHT
In space, the X-wings can manoeuvre and team up against prowling TIE fighters. But there is no room to manoeuvre in the trench leading to the exhaust port, leaving the rebel pilots dangerously unprotected.

**VEHICLE**

Darth Vader's TIE Fighter

## STUDYING THE CLASSICS
- As a guide for his visual effects team, Lucas edited together footage of a dogfight, using scenes from classic war films such as *The Dam Busters*, *The Bridges at Toko-Ri*, and *Tora! Tora! Tora!*

The X-wing's oversized laser cannons let the fighter's weapons operate at longer range.

**LUKE, BIGGS AND WEDGE** streak down the trench, flying full-throttle to keep Vader and his wingmen off their backs. But the Sith Lord closes in, driving off Wedge, killing Biggs and damaging R2-D2. Luke is alone – and the rebel cause is in peril. Just then, Han Solo comes streaking into the fight to even the odds, blasting the fighters and sending a furious Vader spinning off into deep space, unable to rejoin the fight. Luke takes aim at the Death Star's exhaust port, trusting in the Force.

### A HELPING HAN

Darth Vader closes in – but Han Solo has decided to join the fight. The *Falcon* blasts one TIE fighter and the other two collide, leaving Luke all clear to take his shot.

# TRENCH RUN

**IV** A NEW HOPE

Luke uses his helmet microphone to assure the rebel base he switched off the targeting computer on his X-wing intentionally.

## FAITH IN THE FORCE
Obi-Wan's voice tells Luke to let go and use the Force. To the astonishment of the other rebels, he shuts off his targeting computer. Guided by the Force, he fires at the exhaust port. It's a hit!

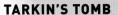

## TARKIN'S TOMB
The Death Star explodes in a gigantic fireball ending Grand Moff Tarkin's schemes. Luke hears Obi-Wan's voice again, "Remember the Force will be with you, always."

## IF AT FIRST...
- Lucas wrote separate scenes in which Luke makes another trench run, missing the exhaust port on his first attempt, then abandoning his targeting computer the second time round. The sequences were combined to speed up the story.

Targeting computers count down the range to the exhaust port so pilots know when to fire torpedoes.

## "You're all clear, kid! Now let's blow this thing and go home!"
HAN SOLO

**THE DESTRUCTION** of the Death Star is an enormous victory for the Rebel Alliance and a critical blow for freedom in the galaxy. The rebels celebrate by giving medals to the heroes of the Battle of Yavin – led by Luke Skywalker, who has taken his first steps towards learning the ways of the Force and claiming his Jedi heritage. However, Darth Vader has escaped to tell the Emperor that his planet-killing weapon is no more. The rebels have won a key fight, but the Empire will strike back.

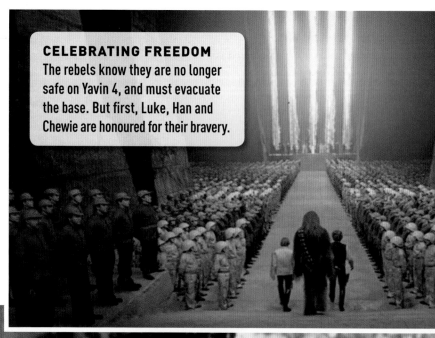

**CELEBRATING FREEDOM**
The rebels know they are no longer safe on Yavin 4, and must evacuate the base. But first, Luke, Han and Chewie are honoured for their bravery.

Though badly damaged in the battle, R2-D2 is repaired in time for the celebration.

# VICTORY AT YAVIN

IV A NEW HOPE

## A SMUGGLER'S LOYALTIES

The rebels would have perished without Han. As Leia gives the smuggler his medal, she hopes he will now want to help save the galaxy, and not just his own skin.

## MISSION COMPLETE

C-3PO thinks danger and excitement are bad ideas, but R2-D2 takes satisfaction in having completed his mission, and looks forward to new adventures with Luke and his friends.

General Dodonna is one of the Alliance's most respected military commanders.

## OVERDUE HONOUR

- Hey, where's Chewie's medal? He got one in the novelisation of *A New Hope*, in a 1980 comic book, and most famously from actress Carrie Fisher at the 1997 MTV Movie Awards.

**THREE YEARS AFTER** the destruction of the Death Star, the Rebel Alliance is once more on the run. Driven from their base on Yavin 4, the rebels have been hunted across the galaxy by the Sith Lord Darth Vader and Imperial warships. The rebels have built their new Echo Base on the planet Hoth, hoping that the Empire will fail to detect their presence on the remote planet. But the Emperor's servants have sent thousands of probe droids to find them – and Hoth has dangers of its own.

## THE WILDS OF HOTH

Luke Skywalker is investigating what he thinks is a meteor strike when his tauntaun steed grows agitated. Camouflaged by the snow until it strikes, a wampa kills the tauntaun and drags Luke away.

# WAMPA ATTACK

## CHANGE OF PLANS

- A subplot involving wampas invading the Rebel Alliance base was cut when the creatures did not prove convincing.

- 1997's special edition (theatrical version) replaced the original wampa with a digital version of the beast.

> Luke does not try to use his comlink because the sound would alert the wampa.

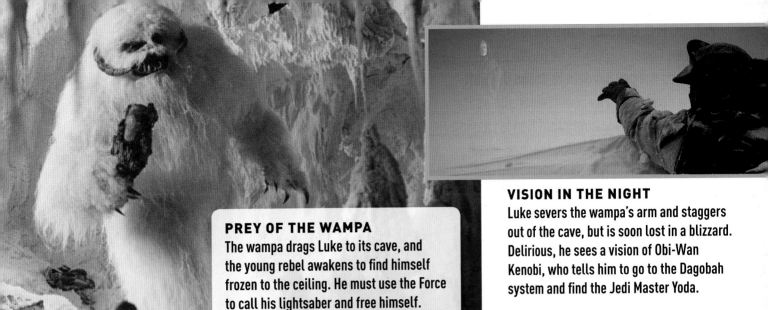

### PREY OF THE WAMPA
The wampa drags Luke to its cave, and the young rebel awakens to find himself frozen to the ceiling. He must use the Force to call his lightsaber and free himself.

### VISION IN THE NIGHT
Luke severs the wampa's arm and staggers out of the cave, but is soon lost in a blizzard. Delirious, he sees a vision of Obi-Wan Kenobi, who tells him to go to the Dagobah system and find the Jedi Master Yoda.

### DROID

Treadwell Droid

### LOCATIONS

Hoth

Echo Base

### CREATURES

Tauntaun

Wampa

To move an object, a Jedi must feel the Force between himself and his target.

### "There isn't enough life on this ice cube to fill a space cruiser."
HAN SOLO

**AT ECHO BASE,** Han Solo tells Rebel Alliance General Rieekan he has to leave: if Han does not pay his debt to Jabba the Hutt he is a dead man. The commander allows it, but Princess Leia is angry that Han is running off when the Alliance needs leaders – and angrier still when Han says she could use a good kiss. Before Han can repair the *Millennium Falcon*, however, he learns that Luke has not returned from his patrol. Han knows Luke cannot survive a freezing night outside the base, so he rides off to find him.

### A REBEL IN TROUBLE

Han finds Luke near death, and knows he must work quickly to save both their lives. Back at Echo Base, the rebels can no longer wait for the missing men to return. They close the shield doors until morning.

# RESCUE ON HOTH

Jabba put a price on Han's head after the smuggler failed to repay him for cargo Han dumped when caught smuggling by Imperial officials.

### HOTEL HOTH

- Scenes of Luke staggering through the snow were filmed just metres from the crew's hotel in Finse, Norway.

- Legendary *Star Wars* artists Ralph McQuarrie and Joe Johnston have cameos as soldiers at Echo Base.

## STRANGE SHELTER
When Han's tauntaun dies from cold, the smuggler takes Luke's lightsaber and slices open the creature's belly, sliding his friend inside. It smells awful, but it will keep Luke warm while Han sets up a shelter for the night.

## LUKE'S RECOVERY
A snowspeeder pilot finds the missing rebels in the morning. Immersion in healing bacta enables Luke to recover from his ordeal.

### VEHICLE

Snowspeeder

### NOTABLE CHARACTERS

General Rieekan  Zev Senesca

### DROIDS

2-1B  FX-7

Rebel engineers used laser ice-cutters to enlarge caverns and create passages.

> "I'd just as soon kiss a Wookiee."
> **PRINCESS LEIA**

THE METEOR THAT Luke was unable to investigate turns out to be an Imperial probe droid, which spies on the rebels before Han and Chewie can destroy it. When Darth Vader sees the droid's report, he senses the rebels are on Hoth – and that the boy who destroyed the Death Star is with them. The rebels have only just established Echo Base, but General Rieekan knows they cannot stay. He orders them to begin evacuating their base as Vader's Star Destroyers race towards Hoth.

**UNFRIENDLY VISITOR**
Responding to a distress call, Han destroys the prowling droid. But it is too late: the robot has transmitted its data to the Empire.

## VADER'S SEARCH

**NOTABLE CHARACTERS**

Admiral Piett

General Veers

Admiral Ozzel

Berryl Chiffonage

**VEHICLES**

Executor

Imperial Star Destroyer

**DROID**

Probe Droid

The meditation chamber can be closed and pressurised, allowing Vader to breathe without his mask.

## DESTINATION HOTH

Vader's task force, led by the massive *Executor*, emerges from hyperspace in the Hoth system. But the rebels are on alert, and an energy shield protects their base from orbital bombardment.

## PIETT'S PROMOTION

The Empire will have to land ground troops to take the base. Angry about the delay, Vader blames Admiral Ozzel for poor tactics, and strangles him with the Force, promoting Captain Piett to Admiral.

# "You have failed me for the last time, Admiral."

### DARTH VADER

What Vader thinks about inside his chamber is a topic of secret fascination among his officers.

## A BRITISH EMPIRE

- Director Irvin Kershner deliberately gave the Imperials English accents and the rebels American ones. Vader, he explained, was an exception because he "used to be a good guy".

**THE EMPIRE LANDS** AT-AT walkers and they begin to march across Hoth's icy plains, targeting the rebel shield generators and base. Luke and Rogue Squadron's rebel pilots fly out to stop them. When the walkers' armour proves too strong for blasters, Luke suggests tripping their legs using tow cables. But the Rogues realise they have no chance of beating the superior Imperial force. They can only hope to give as many rebels as possible the chance to evacuate before the Empire takes control of the base.

## ORGANA'S ORDERS
Leia gives rebel X-wing pilots a difficult mission: to escort the Alliance's transports past Vader's Star Destroyers, which are in orbit above.

## THE BATTLE OF HOTH

### NOTABLE CHARACTERS

Dak Ralter

Wes Janson

Hobbie Klivian

Captain Lennox

Major Derlin

Hoth's rebels retreat after the AT-ATs break their lines. Few will escape.

### LITTLE BY LITTLE
- The AT-ATs were brought to life through stop-motion animation, with models repositioned slightly after each frame of film. Five seconds of filming required around 120 changes to a model's position.

THE EMPIRE STRIKES BACK

144

## SACRIFICE IN THE SNOW

Rebel soldiers in cold-weather gear hunker down in trenches and defend their base with heavy cannons. However, the walkers' remorseless advance soon overruns the rebels, forcing a retreat.

## HEAVY FOOTSTEPS

A walker shoots down Luke's snowspeeder and nearly crushes him with its giant mechanical foot. Luke manages to destroy one AT-AT, but knows the battle is lost. He heads for his X-wing, where R2-D2 is waiting.

"Go for the legs – it might be our only chance of stopping them."

LUKE SKYWALKER

The AT-AT commander stands in its head, behind the two pilots. Troops deploy from the body.

### VEHICLES

AT-AT

AT-ST

**AS THE EMPIRE** closes in, Han and Chewie try frantically to repair their ship. When Leia and C-3PO are cut off from the last rebel transport, they hitch a ride aboard the *Falcon*. The two smugglers get the *Falcon* working, narrowly escaping Vader and his snowtroopers, but are pursued by Star Destroyers and a swarm of TIE fighters. Han needs every trick in the flight manual to keep them off his tail, and is far too busy to stop and hear whatever it is that C-3PO keeps trying to tell him.

### IMPERIAL INVADERS
Leaving Chewie to get the *Falcon* spaceworthy, Han finds Leia still in the Echo Base command centre. She refuses to leave her post – until she hears that Imperial troops have entered the base.

# IMPERIAL PURSUIT

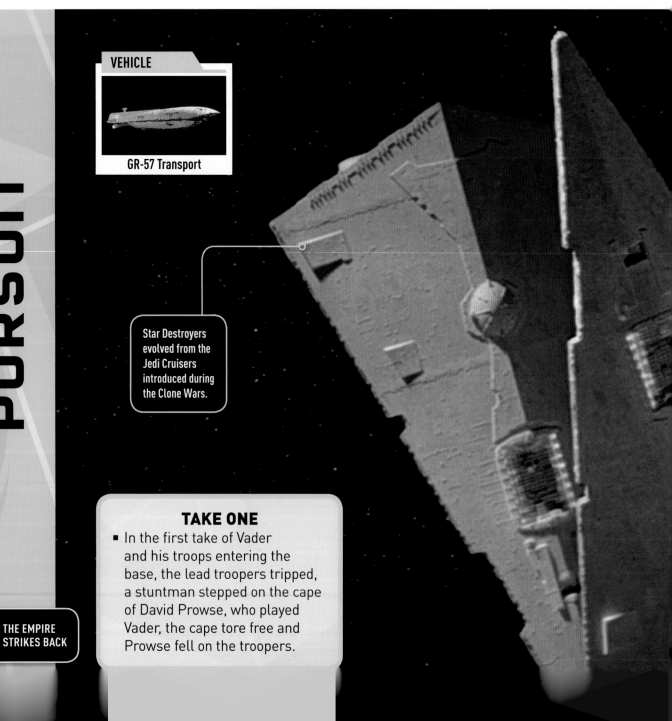

**VEHICLE**

GR-57 Transport

Star Destroyers evolved from the Jedi Cruisers introduced during the Clone Wars.

### TAKE ONE
- In the first take of Vader and his troops entering the base, the lead troopers tripped, a stuntman stepped on the cape of David Prowse, who played Vader, the cape tore free and Prowse fell on the troopers.

V THE EMPIRE STRIKES BACK

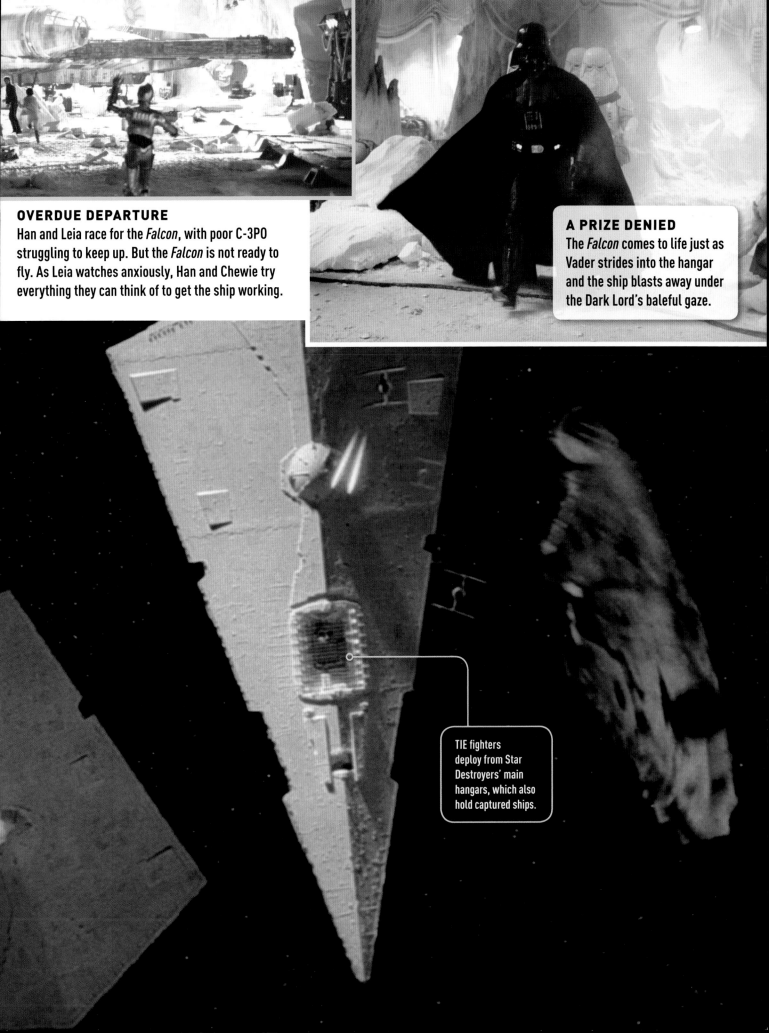

## OVERDUE DEPARTURE
Han and Leia race for the *Falcon*, with poor C-3PO struggling to keep up. But the *Falcon* is not ready to fly. As Leia watches anxiously, Han and Chewie try everything they can think of to get the ship working.

## A PRIZE DENIED
The *Falcon* comes to life just as Vader strides into the hangar and the ship blasts away under the Dark Lord's baleful gaze.

TIE fighters deploy from Star Destroyers' main hangars, which also hold captured ships.

**POOR C-3PO KEEPS** trying to tell Han something important: he has noticed that the *Falcon*'s hyperdrive has been damaged. Han discovers this for himself when he tries to go into lightspeed and escape the ship's pursuers. When another round of hasty repairs fails to fix the problem, Han takes the freighter into an asteroid field, dodging huge flying chunks of rock. Several TIE fighters are destroyed trying to follow them, but it takes all of Han's skills as a pilot for the *Falcon* and her passengers to avoid the same fate.

### "SOMETHING HIT US!"

Han and Chewie are trying to figure out what's wrong with the *Falcon*'s hyperdrive motivator when an impact rattles the freighter. Han knows it is no laser blast – the *Falcon* has hit something.

## INTO THE ASTEROIDS

**LOCATION**

Hoth Asteroid Belt

TIE fighters lack shields, making passage through an asteroid field suicidal.

Some asteroids contain mineral wealth or are used as bases, but others are just a navigational nuisance.

### ROCKY ROAD
The *Falcon* has collided with a small asteroid. Hoping to shake the Imperials, Han heads into the chaotic swirl of tumbling rocks.

### A HIDING SPOT
It is a terrifying journey, but the smuggler's gamble works. The TIE pilots who follow the *Falcon* smash into the rocks, giving Han a chance to hide the damaged *Falcon* in a particularly large asteroid's deep cave.

## "You don't have to do this to impress me."
### PRINCESS LEIA

### POTATO PERIL
- Some of the asteroids in the background of these shots are actually potatoes.
- Visual effects cameraman Ken Ralston's love of classic cartoons inspired many of the dizzying camera movements in the asteroid chase.

**WITH THE FORCE** to guide him, Luke flies his X-wing to Dagobah to search for Yoda, as instructed by his vision of Obi-Wan Kenobi. He crashes into a swamp and sets up a rough camp amid the muck of the swamp world. A frustrated Luke has no idea how to find the mysterious Jedi Master he is seeking, but he does get help from a strange little green visitor who investigates his camp – and claims to know Yoda. As an impatient Luke will soon discover, on Dagobah things are rarely what they seem.

## MAROONED REBEL

Luke's arrival on Dagobah does not go exactly as he planned: his X-wing winds up in a murky bog, and a swamp creature nearly eats R2-D2. This seems like a strange place to find a Jedi Master.

## JEDI QUEST

During the Clone Wars, Yoda visited Dagobah at the urging of the spirit of Qui-Gon Jinn.

### "Much anger in him, like his father."

YODA

### FINDING YODA

- The filmmakers considered many approaches to Yoda, including putting a mask on a monkey, before settling on a puppet created by Stuart Freeborn and operated by a team led by Frank Oz. In early story drafts Yoda was known as "Minch-Yoda".

THE EMPIRE STRIKES BACK

## UNEXPECTED GUIDE
Luke is annoyed when an odd creature arrives at his camp and begins rummaging through his supplies. But the new arrival claims he will take Luke to Yoda, and beckons him deeper into the steamy swamplands.

## THE MASTER REVEALED
When Luke's impatience boils over, the creature sighs, and they hear the voice of Obi-Wan. Luke's guide is Yoda himself!

R2-D2 recharges from a portable power generator Luke brought in his X-wing.

**BACK ABOARD VADER'S** Star Destroyer, Admiral Piett tells the Dark Lord that Emperor Palpatine demands to speak with him. Retreating to his private chamber, Vader contacts the Emperor, who is also the Sith Lord Darth Sidious. Palpatine tells Vader that Luke is the son of Anakin Skywalker, Vader's former self, and warns that Luke could destroy them. Vader reminds him that Luke could be a powerful ally if turned to the dark side, and vows Luke will join the Sith or die.

### RIGHT HAND OF THE EMPEROR
To officers like Admiral Piett, Vader is the Emperor's feared enforcer, carrying out his orders with brutal efficiency. Few in the Empire know that the two are Sith Master and apprentice.

# THE SON OF SKYWALKER

### EYES OF THE EMPEROR
- George Lucas turned to Ian McDiarmid and James Earl Jones to rework this scene for the 2004 DVD release. The original Emperor was voiced by Clive Revill and played by a masked Elaine Baker, with chimpanzee eyes superimposed over her own.

> ## "The son of Skywalker must not become a Jedi."
> **EMPEROR PALPATINE**

Vader's chamber aboard the *Executor* is shielded to keep sensitive communications secret.

**V**  THE EMPIRE STRIKES BACK

**NOTABLE CHARACTER**

**Emperor Palpatine**

## WEB OF THE SITH
Betrayal is the way of the Sith and ensures that the strong triumph. Sidious constantly tests Vader, and Vader seeks to undermine Sidious. Luke's growing power is a new element in their endless competition.

### THE LOST CHILD
Vader was led to believe his child died with Padmé. He questions how it is possible that the Rebel Alliance hero Luke Skywalker might be the son he lost many years ago.

Sidious's aim is to ensnare Luke Skywalker and make him his new Sith apprentice, replacing Vader.

THE *FALCON* IS safe for the moment from her Imperial pursuers, giving Han and Chewbacca a chance to fix her ailing hyperdrive. In the quiet asteroid cave that serves as the ship's hiding place, Han's thoughts increasingly turn to Princess Leia, who finally allows herself to admit that she is attracted to the man she sometimes puts down as a scoundrel. But Imperial bombers are hunting for the *Falcon*, and the hidden cave turns out to pose dangers even worse than the perils of the asteroid field.

**ROMANTIC INTERLUDE**
When Han takes Leia's hand, she surrenders to the moment, kissing him before C-3PO interrupts their embrace.

**IN THE DARK**
- C-3PO's interruption of the kiss was an ad lib invented during shooting.

- In scenes showing the *Falcon* repairs, Irvin Kershner showed so much welding because that was easier for the audience to see in the darkness than other repairs the *Falcon* might have needed.

# DANGEROUS HIDE AWAY

"No time to discuss this in committee!"

HAN SOLO

**CREATURES**

Space Slug

Mynock

**VEHICLE**

TIE Bomber

THE EMPIRE STRIKES BACK

## MYNOCK HUNT
Later, Leia spots mynocks in the cave, and joins Han and Chewie to burn the power-draining pests off the ship. When a blaster bolt misses, the entire cave shudders. Caves are not supposed to do that!

## "THIS IS NO CAVE!"
Han fires up the *Falcon*'s engines, ignoring Leia's protests and his worries about the hyperdrive. His ship is inside the gullet of a massive space slug! They escape just in time.

The asteroid field overlaps the boundaries of the neighbouring Hoth and Anoat star systems.

Sightings of space slugs are usually dismissed as tall tales. Han will have a great story to tell – if he survives.

**ON DAGOBAH, YODA** proves a wise but tough teacher of the Jedi arts, who tries to teach Luke to feel the Force and to control both his powers and the emotions driving them. Like his father before him, Luke proves a stubborn student. He learns his hardest lesson in a cave that draws on fear. Luke ignores Yoda's advice not to take his weapons with him, and encounters an apparition of Darth Vader. He draws his lightsaber and defeats the dark figure, but has a disturbing vision of a potential future.

### JEDI TRAINING
Yoda pushes Luke hard both physically and mentally. He tries to get him to unlearn his responses and open himself to the Force, shedding emotions that cloud his judgment.

# VISION OF THE DARK SIDE

The cave can create visions from minds that give power to that which they fear.

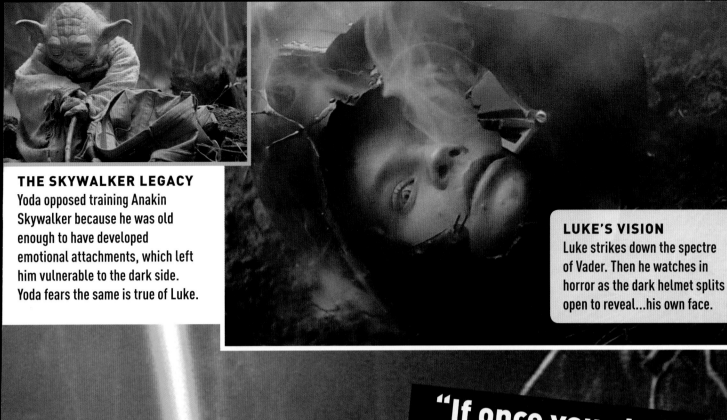

### THE SKYWALKER LEGACY

Yoda opposed training Anakin Skywalker because he was old enough to have developed emotional attachments, which left him vulnerable to the dark side. Yoda fears the same is true of Luke.

### LUKE'S VISION

Luke strikes down the spectre of Vader. Then he watches in horror as the dark helmet splits open to reveal...his own face.

> ## "If once you start down the dark path, forever will it dominate your destiny."

YODA

Facing what he thinks is his father's killer, Luke quickly gives in to fear and hatred.

### ACTING CHALLENGE

- Acting is a collaboration, which made the Dagobah scenes a tough task for Mark Hamill. For the most part he was alone: R2-D2 was remote-controlled and Frank Oz was beneath the sets. Furthermore, he could not hear most of Yoda's lines.

**VADER SUMMONS** bounty hunters, including Boba Fett, to the *Executor*. There, he promises them a substantial reward if they find the *Millennium Falcon* and capture her passengers alive. Fett and the other hunters leave to search for the missing freighter, but it seems that their services might not be needed after all: Admiral Piett reports that Captain Needa of the Star Destroyer *Avenger* has the *Falcon* in his sights, with a squadron of TIE fighters in hot pursuit of the fleeing freighter.

### THE BEST DEFENCE...
When the *Falcon*'s hyperdrive fails again, Han turns the ship around and charges the *Avenger*, just missing her bridge. But to Captain Needa's puzzlement, the freighter then disappears from his warship's scopes.

# THE HUNTERS

IG-series droids such as IG-88 were used as both bodyguards and assassins in the Republic's last years.

## "I want them alive. No disintegrations."
**DARTH VADER**

## A HUNTER ALWAYS KNOWS HIS PREY

It is standard procedure for the *Avenger* to dump her garbage before entering hyperspace, letting the *Falcon* detach and drift away. But Boba Fett knows this trick – and, unknown to Han, is on the *Falcon*'s tail.

## CORELLIAN GAMBLE

Han attaches the *Falcon* to the back of the *Avenger*'s conning tower. Here the giant warship's scanners cannot detect her.

Bossk is a Trandoshan from the same star system as the Wookiees.

### NOTABLE CHARACTERS

Boba Fett

Dengar

IG-88

Bossk

Zuckuss

4-LOM

## SNEAK PREVIEW

- Before Episode V, Boba Fett appeared in the infamous late-1978 *Star Wars* Holiday Special TV show and as an action figure available by post. But his true debut was 24 September 1978, when he marched with Vader at the San Anselmo, California, Country Fair Parade.

LUKE CONTINUES TO learn the ways of the Jedi in the jungles of Dagobah, and is amazed when Yoda levitates his X-wing from the depths of the swamp, setting it gently on the shore. Luke's own power is growing, but he still struggles with overpowering emotions. Meditating with the Force, he sees a city in the clouds where Han and Leia are in pain. When Yoda tells him it is the future he sees, Luke needs to make a choice – continue his training, or rush to help his friends without knowing the consequences.

## A QUESTION OF BELIEF

Luke is dismayed to find his X-wing sinking deeper into the swamp, and is convinced he will never leave Dagobah. Yoda scolds him for his lack of faith, urging him to feel the Force around him and understand that size matters not.

# LUKE'S DECISION

## "Do. Or do not. There is no try."

YODA

In exile, Yoda has lived surrounded by plants and beasts. This simple life has taught the Jedi the fundamental lesson of the Force: life creates it and makes it grow.

**V** THE EMPIRE STRIKES BACK

**LESSON IN THE FORCE**

Challenged by Yoda, Luke tries to levitate his ship, but fails. The Jedi Master then calmly frees the X-wing, and Luke confesses that he does not believe it. Yoda just nods. "That is why you fail," he says.

**JEDI FAREWELL**

Luke departs, promising to return. A despairing Obi-Wan says Luke was the last hope of the Jedi. But Yoda says there is another.

Like many apprentices, Luke must learn to hear the will of the Force rather than try to command it.

**RETURN OF THE JEDI**

- An elderly Alec Guinness agreed to appear in Episode V late in filming, and performed his scenes in a single day.

- Additional shots of the Dagobah swamp were filmed in George Lucas's swimming pool while it was being installed.

**AFTER A LONG** journey, the *Falcon* arrives at Bespin, where Han's old rival Lando Calrissian is the administrator of a mining colony called Cloud City. Lando is angry that Han swindled him last time they met, but appears ready to let bygones be bygones, welcoming his visitors and promising that his technicians will repair the *Falcon*. But something is not right. C-3PO goes missing and is found in a junkpile, while Han, Leia and Chewie discover that Lando has other guests.

## LOW PROFILE

Lando used to own the *Falcon*, but lost her to Han in a wager that may or may not have been fair. He now wants to be a respectable businessman, though he would prefer to avoid attention from the Empire.

# BETRAYAL AT BESPIN

## NOTABLE CHARACTERS

Lando Calrissian

Lobot

E-3PO

### DELAYED DEBUT

- Cloud City was originally imagined for Episode IV, as an Imperial prison in the skies of Alderaan. Budget cuts forced the prison to be combined with the Death Star, bumping Cloud City to a new role in Episode V.

## "We would be honoured if you would join us."
### DARTH VADER

## LOCATIONS

Bespin

Cloud City

## VEHICLE

Cloud Car

## UNPLEASANT SURPRISE
What Lando cannot reveal is that Fett and Vader arrived just before the *Falcon*. They firmly insist that Lando cooperate with them by trapping his old friend.

## NO CONTEST
When Lando brings his guests before Vader, Han draws his blaster and tries to gun down the Dark Lord. Vader disarms him with the Force – Han, Leia and Chewie are now his prisoners.

The *Falcon* needed several weeks to limp from Anoat to Bespin with her backup hyperdrive.

A cybernetic implant allows Lando's aide Lobot to communicate wordlessly with Cloud City's central computer.

**VADER TORMENTS** Han and Leia, but his real target is Luke. The others are simply bait to lure Luke into his trap. Lando is increasingly frustrated as Vader keeps giving him new orders, but he still hopes to prevent an Imperial takeover of Cloud City and to protect Leia and Chewie. The Sith Lord decides he will freeze Luke in carbonite before taking him to the Emperor. But when Lando warns that the freezing process might prove fatal, Vader announces he will test it first – on Han Solo.

### A LAST KISS
Chewie fights the stormtroopers, but Han calms his best friend down, reminding him that he has to protect Princess Leia. Han and Leia share a last kiss before Vader's troopers separate them – perhaps forever.

**NOTABLE CHARACTER**

Captain Bewil

**LOCATION**

Carbon-Freeze Chamber

Carbonite is a tough alloy used to transport the volatile Tibanna gas harvested on Bespin.

THE FATE OF HAN SOLO

V THE EMPIRE STRIKES BACK

### CARBON FREEZE
As Vader watches, Han is lowered into the carbon-freezing pit and vanishes behind a curtain of steam. All wait to see if he survived.

### VADER'S TRAP
Han emerges, encased in solid carbonite – and alive. Vader tells Fett to take his prize to Jabba the Hutt and orders Lando to take Leia and Chewbacca to his ship. Then he tells his troops to prepare for Luke's arrival.

When he put a price on Han's head, Jabba did not specify whether it was alive or dead. Fett wonders how the crime lord will feel about "frozen".

## "He's alive – and in perfect hibernation."
LANDO CALRISSIAN

### GET ME A REWRITE
• One of the best-loved exchanges in the saga – Leia saying, "I love you" and Han replying, "I know" – was actor Harrison Ford's idea, the product of a brainstorming session with director Kershner.

**GUIDED BY THE FORCE,** Luke flies to Cloud City. He is soon separated from R2-D2 and lured into the carbon-freezing chamber, where Vader hopes to entomb him for his journey to the Emperor. When Luke sees the black-armoured figure of Vader, he walks confidently up the stairs and looks him in the eye. He is eager to confront the Sith Lord he blames for the deaths of Obi-Wan and his father. The two ignite their lightsabers, and the duel between Jedi and Sith begins.

### VADER'S PRISONERS
Leia catches sight of Luke and tries desperately to warn him that he is walking into a trap. But Luke has come too far to turn back now.

# DUEL A DARK LORD

> "The Force is with you, young Skywalker. But you are not a Jedi yet."
>
> DARTH VADER

### MASKED MEN
- For the duel, Vader was played by Bob Anderson, a fencing legend who had coached film star Errol Flynn.
- The Imperial officer who drags Leia off was played by Jeremy Bulloch, who also portrayed Boba Fett.

**V** THE EMPIRE STRIKES BACK

## THE DARK LORD WAITS

Face to face with Luke Skywalker at last, Darth Vader allows himself a moment of satisfaction. He will test the boy to determine what he has learned and how powerful he might become.

## LIGHT AND DARK

Luke proves an impressive opponent, displaying Jedi reflexes in escaping the carbonite and controlling his anger. But Luke has yet to face the full power of the dark side – or discover its secrets.

Luke is not able to remember Obi-Wan's warning not to give in to hate when he finally faces Darth Vader.

Vader is skilled with a lightsaber, though his mechanical arms prevent him from creating Force lightning.

**VADER ATTACKS LUKE** in a fury, driving his opponent onto a narrow gantry within Cloud City's reactor shaft. Luke cannot match the relentless power of the Sith Lord, and must retreat until cornered. When Luke continues his resistance, Vader chops off his hand, leaving him helpless. The young Jedi is beaten, but to his shock Vader does not kill him – he asks Luke to join him. Vader has his own plans for Luke's destiny, and a stunning secret to reveal about the past.

### JEDI DISARMED

Too late, a battered and broken Luke understands why Obi-Wan and Yoda said he was not ready to face Vader. He keeps fighting, but it is hopeless: Vader breaks his defences and severs his hand.

A briefly overconfident Vader let down his guard, allowing Luke to land a glancing blow to his armour.

# DARK LORD'S SECRET

### THE POWER OF THE DARK SIDE
A defiant Luke refuses Vader's invitation to complete his training – how could he join the man who killed his father? Vader's response leaves the young Jedi numb with horror: he is Luke's father.

### SURRENDER TO THE FORCE
Despite his agony, Luke senses the truth of Vader's words. He has another choice – to die. He lets go and falls down the reactor shaft.

## "No. I am your father."
### DARTH VADER

Luke and Vader fight in a vast reactor shaft that processes valuable gases.

### KEEPING SECRETS
- Episode V's biggest secret was not shared with Hamill until shortly before this scene was filmed. David Prowse was given "dummy" lines that said Obi-Wan killed Luke's father.

**LANDO CALLS HIS GUARDS** and frees Leia and Chewie, telling them they can still catch Boba Fett before he takes off with Han. The rescue attempt fails, but they find R2-D2 and fight their way to the *Falcon*. As they flee Cloud City, Leia senses Luke calling to her through the Force and knows he is in grave danger. The *Falcon* returns to the underside of Cloud City and plucks Luke from his perch. Vader's ship is waiting for them, however, and his troops have deactivated the *Falcon*'s hyperdrive.

### LUKE'S CALL
Luke is sucked out of the reactor shaft and left hanging above the clouds of Bespin. Trapped and nearly broken by Vader's revelation, he reaches out through the Force for help.

# LANDO'S CONSCIENCE

> "We're getting out of here."
> **LANDO CALRISSIAN**

### NO SUBSTITUTE
- Actor Peter Mayhew was ill one day and Irvin Kershner shot scenes with a replacement. But without Mayhew in Chewie's costume, the Wookiee's body language looked wrong and the footage was scrapped.

## HUNTER'S PRIZE
Boba Fett departs for Tatooine before Leia can save Han. But the princess refuses to be beaten. She manages to escape from Cloud City – and then finds there is one dear friend she can still save.

## R2-D2 TO THE RESCUE
The *Falcon* saves Luke, but her hyperdrive is still broken. R2-D2 claims he knows what is wrong. Can the little droid save the day?

In different circumstances, Lando would enjoy returning to the freighter he lost to Han in a game of sabacc.

Imperial technicians have undone the repairs made to the *Falcon*, leaving her unable to enter hyperspace.

**R2-D2 FIXES** the hyperdrive and the *Falcon* escapes, leaving Vader to brood about his failure to win his son over to the dark side. The rebels have suffered a terrible defeat, and must regroup. Luke has discovered the dark secret of his birth, and knows he is not yet able to defeat the Sith. Han is a captive on his way to Jabba the Hutt. But Luke has been given a mechanical hand, and the Rebel Alliance has survived – its fight for freedom will go on.

**VADER'S DEFEAT**
When the *Falcon* escapes, Vader's officers fear for their lives. But the Sith Lord stalks away without so much as a glance at his men.

The Rebel Alliance fleet has assembled on the outskirts of the galaxy to escape Imperial hunters.

C-3PO was fitted with this mismatched droid plating sometime after the Clone Wars.

# THE SEARCH FOR SOLO

**V** THE EMPIRE STRIKES BACK

### JEDI REPAIRS

The *Falcon* reaches the rebel fleet, and now Luke's injuries can be treated. A medical droid creates a mechanical hand to replace the one Luke lost on Bespin in his ill-advised duel with Vader.

### PROMISES MADE

Lando and Chewbacca prepare to depart, vowing to find Boba Fett. Luke has made promises of his own: he will rescue Han, then return to Dagobah to finish his Jedi training and fulfill his destiny.

**VEHICLE**

Nebulon-B Frigate

### WITH FEELING

- Kershner showed Luke reacting to his fingers being pricked so the audience would know he had feeling in his mechanical hand.

- In this scene Leia once more wears her outfit from Episode IV.

SIX MONTHS AFTER the Rebel Alliance's devastating defeat on Hoth, it faces a new peril: the Empire has begun construction of a second Death Star – one with twice the power of the battle station destroyed by Luke Skywalker at Yavin. As rebel spies discover the secrets of the new Death Star, Luke, Princess Leia, Lando Calrissian, and Chewie have a mission of their own. They must rescue Han Solo, who is still frozen in carbonite, from the Tatooine palace of the ruthless crime lord Jabba the Hutt.

**DROIDS AT THE DOOR**
To start his plan to rescue Han, Luke sends C-3PO and R2-D2 to call on the Hutt. The droids have a message for Jabba – and a gift.

# THE PALACE OF JABBA THE HUTT

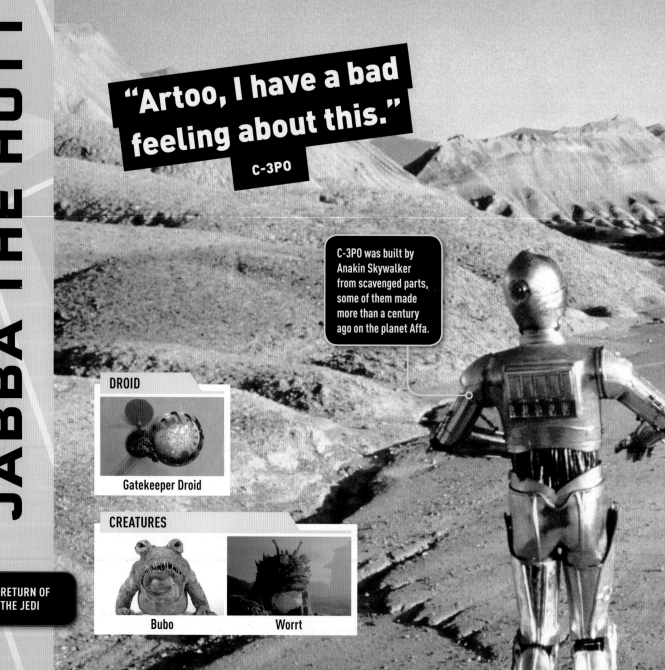

### "Artoo, I have a bad feeling about this."
C-3PO

C-3PO was built by Anakin Skywalker from scavenged parts, some of them made more than a century ago on the planet Affa.

**DROID**

Gatekeeper Droid

**CREATURES**

Bubo

Worrt

## MESSAGE FROM LUKE
R2-D2 plays a hologram of Luke, in which the Jedi seeks a meeting with Jabba to bargain for Han's life. To C-3PO's dismay, Luke ends the message by giving the droids to Jabba as a gesture of good will.

## CRIMINAL COURT
Bib Fortuna, Jabba's valet, presents the droids to his master before a crowd of alien low-lifes, which include the bounty hunter Boba Fett. C-3PO spots the frozen Han hanging on a wall as a decoration.

Luke has built a new lightsaber and hidden it inside R2-D2's dome as part of his plan to save Han.

## AHEAD OF ITS TIME
- In Lucas's early scripts, one potential site for Jabba's palace was a grassy world called Sicemon, which Ralph McQuarrie conceptualised. His artwork inspired the planet Lothal in 2014's *Star Wars: Rebels*.

## NOTABLE CHARACTERS

Bib Fortuna          Salacious Crumb          EV-9D9

JABBA SENDS C-3PO and R2-D2 to his dungeons, where R2-D2 is assigned to the Hutt's sail barge and C-3PO is sent back to the throne room as an interpreter. C-3PO must translate when the alien bounty hunter Boushh arrives with a captive Chewbacca. Jabba pays a bounty for Chewie, who is thrown in prison, and invites Boushh to join the depraved party in his palace. But things are not as they seem: Boushh is actually Leia. That night, the princess sheds her disguise and frees Han from his carbonite prison.

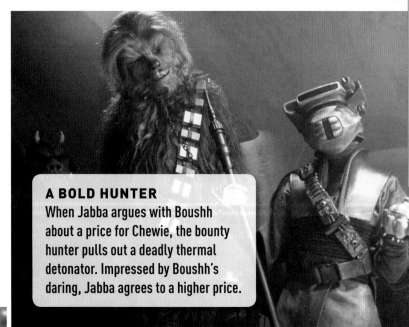

**A BOLD HUNTER**
When Jabba argues with Boushh about a price for Chewie, the bounty hunter pulls out a deadly thermal detonator. Impressed by Boushh's daring, Jabba agrees to a higher price.

**NOTABLE CHARACTER**

Gargan

# THE RESCUE OF HAN SOLO

### ALIEN ORIGINS
- The Jabba the Hutt puppet required four tonnes of clay to sculpt and was animated by three puppeteers on the inside.
- Actress Pat Welsh voiced not only Boushh but also the title character in *E.T.:The Extra-Terrestrial.*

## FREEING HAN

That night, Boushh creeps through the dark throne room and sets Han free from the carbonite. The smuggler has hibernation sickness from his ordeal and cannot see, but he is overjoyed to hear the voice of the woman he loves.

Bib Fortuna is a Twi'lek from the planet Ryloth. Twi'leks have long, flexible "head tails" called lekku.

Leia spots Lando in the crowd, disguised as a guard. But she warns him with a glance not to reveal himself yet.

"We have powerful friends. You're going to regret this."

PRINCESS LEIA

WITH HIS FRIENDS inside Jabba's palace, Luke begins the next part of his plan: bargaining for Han's freedom. Jabba tells Bib Fortuna not to allow the Jedi inside, but Luke uses the Force to cloud Bib's mind. When the same trick fails to work on the strong-willed Hutt, Luke tries to fight – but Jabba hits a hidden switch that sends Luke and an unlucky Gamorrean guard falling through a trap door into a pit below the throne room. The pit holds a monster called the rancor, which gobbles down the guard and then eyes Luke hungrily.

**THE BEAST WITHIN**
In the throne room above, Leia and C-3PO look on in horror. Luke dodges the rancor's attempts to seize him and make him its next meal.

# BEWARE THE RANCOR

**NOT SO FIERCE**
- The roars of the mighty rancor were altered growls made by a dachshund named Max.
- The special effects team used a rod puppet for the rancor after deciding that a man-sized costume looked unconvincing.

**NOTABLE CHARACTERS**

Malakili

Ephant Mon

Hermi Odle

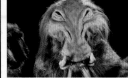
J'Quille

Tessek

## MONSTROUS END
Luke hurls the skull at the gate's control, causing it to fall and kill the unfortunate monster. A furious Jabba decides Luke and his friends will be executed in the Great Pit of Carkoon – which fits Luke's plan.

## QUICK THINKING
The rancor tries to eat Luke, but the Jedi grabs a bone, which he wedges in its jaws. Luke notices that a heavy gate divides the pit into two parts. He grabs a skull and makes one last attempt to save himself.

Gamorrean guards are light on brains but heavy on muscle: they fight for their master with huge axes.

### CREATURE
Rancor

## "Your mind powers will not work on me, boy!"
JABBA THE HUTT

Jabba uses the trap door in his floor to dispose of enemies, disloyal servants and guests who bore him.

**THE GREAT PIT** of Carkoon is the lair of the terrible sarlacc, to which Jabba feeds his prisoners. While Jabba watches from his sail barge, a skiff carrying Luke, Han and Chewie is manoeuvred over the pit. Jabba orders his guards to force Luke into the monster's mouth, but R2-D2 has reached the top deck of the barge – and fires Luke's lightsaber from its hiding place in his dome. To the astonishment of Jabba and his thugs, Luke leaps into the air, grabs his weapon and turns on the stunned guards. The fight is on!

### JEDI PLAN

Away from Jabba's palace, Luke faces much better odds of fighting his way free. He tells Han to stick close to Chewie and the disguised Lando, steps on the plank above the sarlacc and waits for R2-D2.

# THE GREAT PIT OF CARKOON

### NOTABLE CHARACTERS

| | | |
|---|---|---|
| Klaatu | Barada | Vizam (Nikto) |
| Ree-Yees | Saelt-Marae | Pagetti Rook |

### CREATURE

Sarlacc

### VEHICLES

Sail Barge

Skiff

### GANGSTERS END

- Jabba's death echoes that of Luca Brasi, the enforcer in the 1972 classic *The Godfather*.
- Screenwriter Lawrence Kasdan suggested that Lando should die at the sarlacc pit, but that idea was abandoned.

**VI** RETURN OF THE JEDI

The sarlacc swallows its victims whole and digests them over an excruciating 1,000 years – or so legends on Tatooine claim.

## SLAVE'S REVENGE

Luke's attack throws Jabba's goons into a panic. Amid the chaos, Leia wraps her chain across Jabba's throat and chokes the gangster to death.

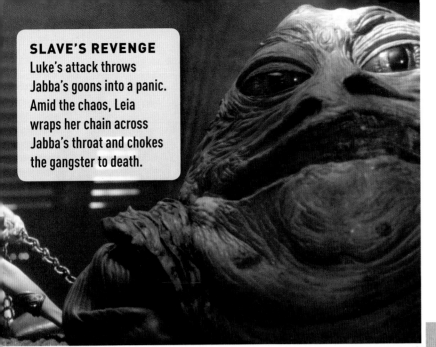

## FREEDOM ON TATOOINE

During the fight, Boba Fett and many of Jabba's thugs plunge into the gaping mouth of the sarlacc. Luke and Leia fire a cannon into the barge, then swing to safety aboard the skiff. The heroes and droids flee as the barge explodes.

"They're going to execute Master Luke – and if we're not careful, us too."

**C-3PO**

Luke wears simple, functional clothing suitable for a Jedi Knight.

ABOVE THE REMOTE planet of Endor, the Empire is building a new Death Star to enforce its will. Emperor Palpatine (the Sith Lord Darth Sidious) arrives on the battle station where he is met by his apprentice Darth Vader. Sidious knows Vader wishes to continue his search for Luke Skywalker, but tells him to be patient – Luke will come to him. When that happens, he says, Vader must bring Luke before Sidious. By working together, the two Sith will be able to turn Luke to the dark side of the Force.

## PLOT AFOOT
Even as the Emperor arrives, rebel spies are working to discover the new Death Star's location. The Rebel Alliance hopes that they can destroy the battle station before it becomes operational.

### NOTABLE CHARACTERS

Sim Aloo

Janus Greejatus

Moff Jerjerrod

### LOCATION

Endor

## CHANGING ROLES
- Moff Jerjerrod is a minor character in Episode VI, but early drafts gave him a far larger role in which he competed with Vader for the Emperor's favour.
- Veteran actor Alan Webb was originally chosen to play the Emperor, but had to withdraw due to poor health and the role went to Ian McDiarmid.

**RESURRECTION OF EVIL**

VI
**RETURN OF THE JEDI**

Sidious's plain cloak is made of rough material – a twisted reflection of the simplicity valued by Jedi.

### AN APPRENTICE'S REBELLION

Vader once hoped Luke would help him overthrow Sidious – that father and son would rule the galaxy. But the man who was once Anakin Skywalker no longer struggles to resist the sinister will of his Sith overlord.

### A MASTER'S VISION

The dark side's power has shown Sidious the will of the Force: Luke will surrender to his anger and strike down his father, Anakin. Sidious believes that Luke will then become his new Sith apprentice.

> "The Emperor is not as forgiving as I am."
>
> DARTH VADER

Nearly all galactic citizens know Sidious only as Palpatine, formerly the galaxy's chancellor and now its Emperor.

WHEN LUKE LEFT Dagobah to try and save his friends on Cloud City, he swore to Yoda that he would return to complete his Jedi training. Keeping that promise, he leaves Tatooine for Dagobah, but finds Yoda is near death. The aged Jedi tells Luke he needs no further training in the ways of the Force, but must confront Darth Vader and Emperor Palpatine to become a true Jedi Knight. Yoda dies, passing into the Force. Shortly after, Obi-Wan Kenobi's spirit tells Luke an astonishing family secret.

**A LAST LESSON**
Luke asks if Darth Vader is indeed his father and Yoda says he is. He then warns Luke not to underestimate the Emperor's power, and to resist anger and fear when he faces the Sith.

# RETURN TO DAGOBAH

### NAME THAT FILM
- To preserve secrecy, Lucasfilm invented a code name for Episode VI, referring to the film as "Blue Harvest".
- Episode VI's actual title was changed from *Revenge of the Jedi* to *Return of the Jedi* in December 1982.

Luke believes Darth Vader still has a spark of good in him, and tells Obi-Wan that he cannot kill his own father.

**VI** RETURN OF THE JEDI

**WITH THE FORCE**
All beings must die, and Yoda's time has come. His body vanishes, becoming one with the Force just as Obi-Wan's did on the Death Star.

**SECRETS IN THE DARK**
As Luke returns to his X-wing, Obi-Wan's spirit appears to him. Obi-Wan blames himself for Anakin Skywalker's fall to the dark side, and tells Luke his other great family secret: Princess Leia is his twin sister.

Obi-Wan warns Luke that his father is now more machine than man.

**"You cannot escape your destiny. You must face Darth Vader again."**
OBI-WAN KENOBI

**MEANWHILE, THE REBEL** fleet plans its attack on the Death Star. The rebels believe the Death Star's weapons are not working yet, though they know that the half-built station is protected by an energy shield generated from Endor's moon. They plan for a commando team to land on the moon and bring down the shield before the rebel fleet arrives and launches starfighters to fly into the Death Star and hit its main reactor. Lando will lead the fighter attack, while Han destroys the shield generator, with Leia, Chewie, Luke and the droids.

## PREPARING FOR BATTLE

Luke returns from Dagobah in time for a briefing aboard a Rebel Alliance cruiser, then joins Han's strike team. They fly a stolen Imperial shuttle through the Imperial warships defending Endor and land on its moon.

# SPEEDER BIKE CHASE

### NOTABLE CHARACTERS

Wicket

Admiral Ackbar

Mon Mothma

General Madine

Orrimaarko

### NEED FOR SPEED

- The illusion of speed in this scene is a clever trick: a cameraman walked through the woods with a Steadicam that filmed one frame per second. Played back at 24 frames per second, a calm stroll looked like a hair-raising ride.

The rebels wear camouflage fatigues to blend in with the lush greenery of Endor's Forest Moon.

### THE CHASE BEGINS
Imperial scouts on speeder bikes spot the rebel commandos. Luke and Leia leap on bikes and chase the scouts through the trees.

### EWOK ENCOUNTER
Luke and Leia manage to destroy the scouts before they can alert the Empire, but get separated during the chase. The princess is found by Wicket, a native Ewok warrior. He decides to take her to his village.

The strike team wear protective helmets and survival gear, and carry muffled blasters, rifles and powerful detonators.

**VEHICLES**

Speeder Bike

Mon Calamari Star Cruiser

"You're a jittery little thing, aren't you?"
PRINCESS LEIA

**HAN TELLS THE** rebel commandos to meet him at the shield generator, then goes off with Luke, Chewie and the droids to search for Leia. Their search has barely begun when they are caught in a trap set by the Ewoks and surrounded by the furry warriors. Han reacts angrily, but Luke convinces him not to resist. Luke senses that these natives may be of service. The Ewoks could be valuable allies in carrying out the rebels' vital mission to destroy the shield protecting the Death Star in orbit above.

## GOLDEN GOD

The Ewoks think C-3PO is a deity, and construct a ceremonial chair to carry him to their village in the trees. C-3PO rather enjoys this honour, though his friends – particularly R2-D2 – find it amusing.

# CAPTIVES OF THE EWOKS

### NOTABLE CHARACTERS

Paploo

Teebo

Logray

Chief Chirpa

Leektar

Lumat

### LOCATION

Bright Tree Village

> **"Hey! Point that thing someplace else."**
>
> HAN SOLO

### BEAR ESSENTIALS

- Star Wars veteran Kenny Baker first played Wicket, but 11-year-old Warwick Davis took over the role after Baker fell ill one day.

- The creature effects crew tried and failed to get the Ewoks to blink convincingly, an effect achieved digitally for 2011's Blu-ray release.

Ewoks hunt small forest animals with spears, snaring larger game in nets woven from thick vines and rope.

## FLYING DEITY
Luke levitates C-3PO with the Force, scaring the Ewoks into freeing the rebels. The warriors later agree to join the fight against the Empire.

## SACRIFICIAL FEAST
Leia is at the Ewok village, but the warriors plan to cook her friends as an offering to C-3PO. When the Ewoks refuse C-3PO's request to free the captives, Luke tells the golden droid to use his magic.

The Ewok tribe dwelling in Bright Tree Village controls this area of Endor Moon.

WHILE HIS FRIENDS recruit the Ewoks to join the attack on the shield generator, Luke finds himself troubled. Through the Force, he can sense Darth Vader nearby, and knows the Sith Lord can sense him too. He also still believes that some spark of Anakin Skywalker remains in Vader, and is determined to free his father from the grip of the dark side of the Force. To avoid endangering his fellow rebels, Luke surrenders to an Imperial scout patrol, claiming he was alone on the strike mission.

### THE PAST REVEALED
Before he departs, Luke tells Leia what he has learned from Obi-Wan: she is his secret sister, the long-lost daughter of Anakin Skywalker.

### NOTABLE CHARACTER

Commander Igar

# "It is too late for me, son."
DARTH VADER

Luke hopes the rebel fleet will destroy the Death Star and kill Vader and the Emperor – even if it means his own death.

**VI** RETURN OF THE JEDI

### REBEL SURRENDER

When he learns Luke has surrendered, Vader takes a shuttle to the Forest Moon of Endor to meet his son. Events are proceeding according to the Emperor's vision: Luke has indeed sought out his lost father.

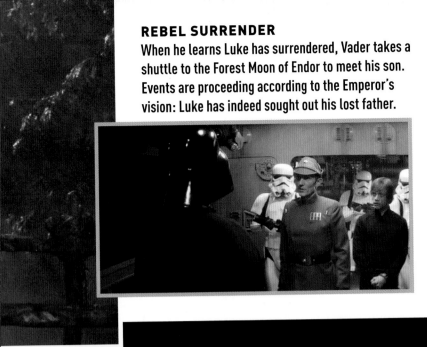

### A SON'S PLEA

Luke addresses Vader as Anakin Skywalker, and urges him to let go of his hate. But Vader reacts angrily to that name. He says Luke must obey the Emperor, and takes his son to the Death Star to face him.

### SITH SUBSTITUTE

- Matte photographer Craig Barron donned Vader's gear for a shot of his arrival on Endor. The problem? Barron was much shorter than David Prowse, who played Vader. He slipped on the cape and fell down the shuttle ramp as onlookers had a good laugh.

This control panel monitors and controls the systems keeping Vader alive within his suit.

**REBEL LEADER** Admiral Ackbar does not know if the strike team has disabled the Death Star's shield, but the attack cannot wait – the Death Star will soon be completed, and killing Emperor Palpatine could bring down the Empire in a single battle. Lando Calrissian leads the rebel fleet through hyperspace to Endor, but horrifying news awaits him. The shield is still up, the Empire is expecting Ackbar's attack and the Death Star's weapons are operational. It seems that Palpatine has lured them into a trap of his own.

### THE BATTLE OF ENDOR
Piloting the *Millennium Falcon*, Lando realises just in time that the Death Star's shield is still up, and barely avoids hitting the energy barrier. But TIE fighters immediately swarm the *Falcon*.

The Death Star's internal systems are mostly complete, but its superstructure is still being assembled.

# SHOWDOWN AT ENDOR

## DESPERATE MEASURES
Lando persuades Ackbar not to break off the attack – the rebels must give Han more time to bring down the energy shield.

### HEAVYWEIGHT FIGHT
Lando knows the Alliance will never have a better chance to defeat the Empire. Rebel and Imperial battleships trade broadsides at close range, with the blasts causing terrible damage.

## "It's a trap!"
### ADMIRAL ACKBAR

### SNEAKY SNEAKER
- Effects wizard Ken Ralston slipped one of his trainers into the background of one complicated shot in the space battle. When production was complete, ILM gave the shoe to producer Howard Kazanjian.

The *Falcon* has been armed with proton torpedos for her attack on the Death Star's main reactor.

### NOTABLE CHARACTERS

Nien Nunb

Ekelarc Yong

Grizz Frix

### VEHICLES

TIE Interceptor

A-Wing Fighter

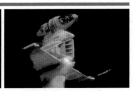

B-Wing Fighter

**HAN AND LEIA** raid the bunker housing the shield generator, but have no idea that the Emperor is aware of the rebel plan – and that an entire legion of crack stormtroopers awaits their team. When troopers backed up by AT-STs capture the rebels, Wicket rushes off to summon the Ewoks, eager to help his friends. The warriors attack the Emperor's troops with spears, stones and bows. The Ewoks lack technology, but they are speedy, stealthy and skilled – and they are defending the forest they love.

## WOOKIEE AND EWOK ATTACK
As the fight in the forest dissolves into chaos, Chewie and two Ewok warriors take control of an AT-ST. The two-legged walker turns the tide, blasting other walkers and squads of stormtroopers.

# FIGHT IN THE FOREST

A stormtrooper confiscates Han's beloved, heavily customised DL-44 pistol.

### NOTABLE CHARACTERS

Widdle

Wunka

Nanta

Romba

Major Newland

Lieutenant Blanaid

### VEHICLE

Ewok Hang Glider

**VI** RETURN OF THE JEDI

## BUNKER BREAK-IN

After several Imperials lock themselves inside the bunker, Leia summons R2-D2 to open the door. When the little droid is hit by a laser blast and disabled, Han tries to bypass the lock's circuitry.

## TARGET DESTROYED

Han succeeds and the rebels wire the bunker with detonators. The blast destroys the shield generator, leaving the Death Star vulnerable.

"Oh my! They'll be captured!"

C-3PO

Projectile weapons cannot penetrate stormtrooper armour, but the underlying body glove offers little protection.

## MISTAKEN IDENTITY

- Because the California woods are supposedly the home of an apelike monster called Bigfoot, which hunters sometimes pursue, actor Peter Mayhew was told not to wander off while in his Chewbacca costume.

## ABOARD THE DEATH STAR,

Emperor Palpatine tries to provoke Luke's anger to make him vulnerable to the dark side of the Force. Luke's fear for his friends is his weakness, so he cannot resist Palpatine's goading. He summons his lightsaber and swings at Vader. Vader blocks the attack, and they duel until Luke regains control of his emotions, deciding not to fight his father. But Vader can read Luke's feelings, and senses that Luke has a twin sister – if his son will not turn to the dark side, perhaps his daughter will.

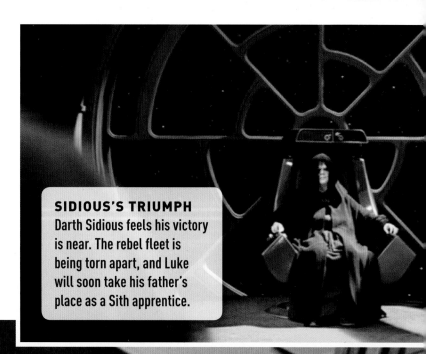

### SIDIOUS'S TRIUMPH
Darth Sidious feels his victory is near. The rebel fleet is being torn apart, and Luke will soon take his father's place as a Sith apprentice.

## DEATH STAR DUEL

### "Good – your hate has made you powerful!"
EMPEROR PALPATINE

### USE THE FORCE
- The scene in which an enraged Luke calls his lightsaber into his hand was shot "backwards" – Mark Hamill made himself look upset, entered the shot as if leaving, looked calm, then threw his weapon away. Then the shot was run in reverse.

Anakin lost his right forearm to Count Dooku long ago. Now, Luke has destroyed the mechanical replacement.

**VI** RETURN OF THE JEDI

### SKYWALKER'S STRUGGLE
Luke tries to awaken Anakin's spirit within Vader, telling his father he can feel the conflict within him. But when Vader senses that Luke has a sister, Luke loses control of his emotions and attacks again.

### JEDI ONSLAUGHT
Luke is angry that Vader might try to turn Leia to the dark side. He batters his father's defences and severs Vader's hand. Darth Sidious's dark-side vision is coming true.

Vader expects neither mercy from his son nor aid from his Master. Betrayal is the Sith way, and the weak are destroyed.

## A DELIGHTED DARTH SIDIOUS

tells Luke to fulfil his destiny and take his father's place. But on the brink of ruin, Luke pulls back, tossing his lightsaber away. He will not strike down the father he had hoped to save, and he will never turn to the dark side. Sidious's plan to gain a new apprentice has failed. The Sith Lord accepts this – but if Luke will not turn, he will be destroyed. Sidious begins to lash Luke with devastating Force lightning. Desperate, the young Jedi calls out to his gravely wounded father for help.

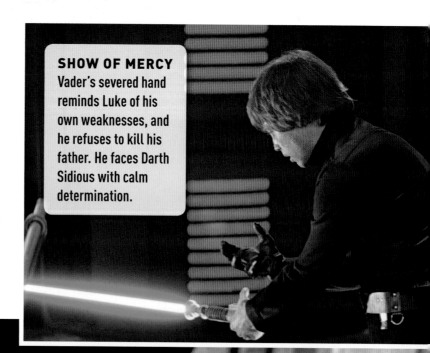

**SHOW OF MERCY**
Vader's severed hand reminds Luke of his own weaknesses, and he refuses to kill his father. He faces Darth Sidious with calm determination.

# CONFRONTING THE EMPEROR

### LIGHTNING FLASHES

- In an early draft the spirits of Obi-Wan and Yoda helped Luke, and their images appeared to deflect the Emperor's lightning.

- Sound designer Ben Burtt recorded sparks made by the props used in the 1931 film *Frankenstein* for the sound of Force lightning.

The Emperor's throne room sits atop a spire high above the Death Star's surface.

> "You've failed, Your Highness. I am a Jedi, like my father before me."
>
> LUKE SKYWALKER

**SITH SORCERY**
Enraged by Luke's defiance, Sidious blasts him with Force lightning – but ignores the injured Vader as he struggles to his feet.

**EMPEROR'S END**
Luke's mercy awakens Vader's love for his lost son. Vader grabs Sidious and hurls him into a bottomless shaft, killing the Sith Lord who destroyed the Jedi, ended the Republic and ruined Anakin Skywalker.

Only the most experienced Jedi masters can resist the malignant, life-draining energies of Force lightning.

**WITH THE SHIELD** that guards the Death Star down, the *Falcon* dives into the battle station's interior, followed by a squadron of rebel starfighters. To buy the fighters time, Ackbar orders his cruisers to attack the command ship *Executor*, which crashes into the Death Star. Inside the battle station, Lando guides the *Falcon* to the main reactor and fires his torpedoes. The dreaded battle station is doomed. But the *Falcon* is now at the heart of Palpatine's terror machine, and it is a long way back to the surface.

### THE TOLL OF WAR

The rebels attack the mighty Super Star Destroyer *Executor*, which meets a fiery end. Ackbar's crew cheer, but Ackbar can only shake his head, appalled by the lives lost on both sides.

# THE SECOND TRENCH RUN

> "Yee-haaa!"
>
> LANDO CALRISSIAN

**NOTABLE CHARACTERS**

Arvel Crynyd

Keir Santage

Jake Farrell

Commander Gherant

## HEART OF DARKNESS
Lando and his co-pilot Nien Nunb lock on to the strongest power source, which leads them to the Death Star's main reactor. They deal the battle station a mortal blow and race to escape.

## VICTORY AT ENDOR
The *Falcon* emerges just before the Death Star explodes into a bright ball of light in the skies of Endor's moon. The Alliance has won!

## DIALECT DOUBLE
- Some of Nien Nunb's lines were in Haya, an African language. Audiences in Kenya were startled to be able to understand Nien's dialogue.

- In early drafts the end battle featured two Death Stars and took place above the Imperial capital, which was then called Had Abbadon.

Wedge Antilles flies using the call sign Red Leader, honouring the squadron that fought at Yavin.

The *Falcon*'s sensor dish is broken off during the trench run.

## BEFORE THE DEATH STAR'S

destruction, Luke carries his wounded father to a shuttle. But Anakin is too badly injured to survive and asks Luke to help him remove his helmet, wanting to see his son without the black mask that has been his face for decades. Then Anakin asks Luke to leave him, but his son refuses, saying he must save his father. Anakin replies that he already has, and dies. A grieving Luke escapes the Death Star and burns his father's black armour in a clearing on the Forest Moon.

**RETURN OF THE JEDI**
Anakin's face is a ruin of burns and scars, but Luke sees past the injuries to his father's humanity. Anakin Skywalker has returned.

Anakin's armour is empty – after his death he passes into the Force, as Obi-Wan and Yoda did before him.

# FAREWELL TO A JEDI

**FAN'S CHOICE**
WITH 67% OF THE TOTAL ONLINE VOTE!

## MORE MAN THAN MACHINE

Anakin's emotional attachments left him vulnerable to the dark side, but also let him break its hold. Luke will remember this lesson as he seeks to rebuild the ranks of the Jedi Order.

## PROPHECY FULFILLED

With Anakin's death, the last remnant of the Sith is no more. The man who helped destroy the Jedi Order also ended the Sith, bringing balance to the Force as prophesied long ago.

## "Just for once, let me look on you with my own eyes."

**ANAKIN SKYWALKER**

### NOTABLE CHARACTER

**Anakin Skywalker**

The funeral pyre leaves no remnant of Darth Vader except ashes and a few scattered bits of plastoid and metal.

## LAST-MINUTE SHOT

- This iconic shot almost did not exist. It was not in the first cut of Episode VI, but editor Duwayne Dunham pointed out that audiences would think Luke left his father aboard the Death Star. The new scene was quickly filmed at Skywalker Ranch in California.

**THE EMPEROR IS DEAD**, the Death Star has been destroyed and the Sith have been defeated. The Rebellion's heroes have won because of their courage under fire, their faith in their friends and their love for each other. And Luke Skywalker has fulfilled his destiny, reigniting the flame of the Jedi and helping his father reclaim his humanity and find peace. As he joins his friends, Luke sees a vision in the Force: the spirits of Obi-Wan Kenobi and Yoda stand beside the redeemed Anakin Skywalker.

## A GALACTIC CELEBRATION

As night falls on the Endor Moon, new explosions fill the sky – but these are fireworks, not weapons. On planets across the galaxy, similar celebrations mark the downfall of the tyrannical Empire.

Anakin's great sacrifice allows him to pass into the Force, appearing as he did before his fall.

# CELEBRATION OF FREEDOM

**VI** RETURN OF THE JEDI

## CIRCLE OF FRIENDS

The Ewok village has never seen such a celebration: Alliance pilots dance with Wookiees and bonfires and victory songs rise into the starry sky.

### HEROES UNITED

The Rebellion's heroes will face new challenges as they work to restore the Republic, but for now they celebrate a hard-won victory.

## GALACTIC CELEBRATION

- The 1997 Special Edition added celebrations on Tatooine, Bespin and Coruscant (in its first film appearance). This idea had been discussed but dropped during preproduction of the original film.

- The 2004 DVD added a celebration on Naboo to the galactic travelogue.

Obi-Wan and Yoda learned to become one with the Force by communicating with Qui-Gon Jinn's spirit.

# ACKNOWLEDGEMENTS

Penguin
Random
House

**Senior Editor** Scarlett O'Hara
**Project Art Editor** Owen Bennett
**Editorial Assistant** Beth Davies
**Pre-Production Producer** Siu Yin Chan
**Producer** Alex Bell
**Managing Editor** Laura Gilbert
**Managing Art Editor** Maxine Pedliham
**Publishing Manager** Julie Ferris
**Art Director** Lisa Lanzarini
**Publishing Director** Simon Beecroft
**Design** Dynamo Limited

**For Lucasfilm**
**Executive Editor** J.W. Rinzler
**Keeper of the Holocron** Leland Chee
**Art Director** Troy Alders
**Director of Publishing** Carol Roeder

Published in Great Britain in 2016 by
Dorling Kindersley Ltd,
80 Strand, London,
WC2R ORL

10 9 8 7 5 4 3 2 1
016-193693-April/2014

A CIP catalogue record for this book is available from
the British Library.

Colour reproduction by Alta Image UK
Printed and bound in China by Leo Paper Products Ltd

ISBN: 978-1-40934-572-5

DK would like to thank Vanessa Bird for the index.

### A WORLD OF IDEAS:
### SEE ALL THERE IS TO KNOW

www.dk.com
www.starwars.com

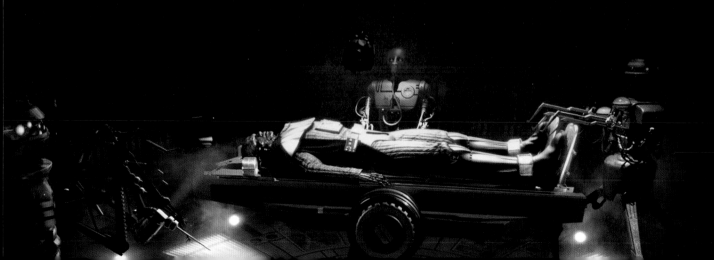